What People Are Saying About Us

"It is a true honor to introduce you to the story within these pages—the raw, deeply honest, and ultimately triumphant journey of Stephen and Krystina Sterne. As their former marriage therapist, I had the privilege of walking alongside them during a pivotal season in their lives. What immediately set Stephen and Krystina apart was not the difficulties they faced—every long-term relationship has them—but their unwavering commitment to meet those difficulties head-on. They weren't just interested in a quick fix; they were determined to fundamentally transform their marriage and their individual selves. Their time in my office was characterized by an intellectual and emotional curiosity that is rare. They leaned into the hard work of self-discovery and mutual understanding. They learned to trace their current struggles back to their family-of-origin experiences, recognizing how past hurts and patterns could surface in their present dynamic. They bravely explored how they communicated, acknowledging that things like withdrawal and anger were often not the problem itself, but shields against feeling unaccepted or controlled. Over time, I witnessed a remarkable shift.

"They moved from a place where emotional walls could be high and conversations could be easily derailed to a place of gentleness and empathy. They committed to slowing down their conversations, learning to truly listen to one another, and to replace criticism and defensiveness with fondness and admiration. They understood that true intimacy is built not on avoiding conflict, but on learning how to repair and reconnect after a fight.

"Perhaps the most impactful phase of their journey was confronting a significant challenge that tested the very foundation of their trust. What I saw during this time was a powerful display of faith, grace, and an extraordinary commitment to forgiveness and healing. Krystina's gentle, yet firm, approach, paired with Stephen's decision to move past shame and guilt toward transparent vulnerability, became the catalyst for a deeper, more resilient bond than they had ever known. They transformed a painful discovery into a shared victory, a testament to their belief that even the darkest secrets can be healed by light. By their final sessions, the metrics of their relationship— their scores on well-known relationship assessments—showed a couple who had not just met but exceeded their original goals. They were flourishing, armed with tools and a mindset to handle whatever life brought next.

"This book is a powerful invitation to witness the courage it takes to become whole—individually and as a couple. Stephen and Krystina have poured their lessons, their vulnerability, and their proven strategies into these pages. If you are looking for a story of real-life struggle, transformative faith, and the tangible steps it takes to build a marriage that is not just intact but thriving, you are in the right hands. Their willingness to share their most difficult moments is a gift to every reader who believes in the power of love, commitment, and hard work.

Read their story. Apply their lessons. Your life and your marriage will be better for it."

—**Brian M, Marriage Counselor (LCSW)**

"We want to express our heartfelt gratitude to Stephen and Krystina for their unwavering commitment to positive change and encouragement throughout this journey. Their transparency and genuine kindness have not only inspired us but have also touched the lives of many around them. With God at the center of their lives, they exemplify the true meaning of service to humanity. Thank you for being beacons of light and love, reminding us all of the power of compassion. This book is a testament to the impact you both have made in my life and the lives of others."

—**Jack and April T, Entrepreneurs, Speakers, Trainers**

"We have shared attending the same church and business community with Stephen and Krystina. They have a heart for the Lord and a burning desire to help people grow in all areas of life. This book contains the best of them as they boldly and transparently share their story with you. It is a true honor to call them friends."

—**Tyler and Amanda S, Entrepreneurs**
and author of *Daily Wins: 31 Day Devotional*

"Stephen and Krystina are one of the most caring and loving couples I know. They've been incredible friends to us through both ups and downs. Their love for others is evident in every relationship they have, but it shines brightest in the way they love each other. Every time I'm around them, I'm inspired to love my own wife even more. Steve's love for Krystina is a powerful example of what it means to love your wife well. I'm grateful to know such a wonderful couple."

—Alec and Morgan H, Real Estate Developer

"Stephen and Krystina are the real deal. Their story is raw, redemptive, and full of God's grace. I've watched them walk through seasons that would have broken many - but instead, they've allowed God to use their pain to bring healing, not just to themselves, but now to countless others. If you've ever wondered if restoration is possible, if love can really be rebuilt, or if God still writes new stories out of broken ones - this book will remind you that He absolutely does."

—Tyler and Alex G, Pastor

Stephen and Krystina are the living definition of a marriage that grows deeper and stronger through every season of life. Their relentless commitment to personal growth and to pouring that growth into one another shines through in every conversation, every glance, every act of service.

Over the years, they've become far more than friends—they've become mentors who let us watch, up close, what it looks like to love and serve your spouse better today than you did yesterday. My wife and I turn to them first whenever we need wisdom about marriage, because their relationship isn't just advice they give; it's the daily, visible fruit of a love that keeps choosing the other person, every single day.

—**Dr. Flint & Rachel S, D.C.**

Over the years, they've become far more than friends—they've

Grace Even After

A Love Redeemed, A Hope Restored

STEPHEN AND KRYSTINA STERNE

Grace Even After: A Love Redeemed, A Hope Restored
© 2025 by Stephen and Krystina Sterne
www.graceevenafter.com

ALL RIGHTS RESERVED

Published by

Ssali Publishing House

Ssali Publishing House

Because Everyone Has a Story Worth Telling!

In Proud Collaboration with

UNISA university of south africa PRESS

ISBN: 978-0-473-76967-3

TABLE OF CONTENTS

Part IV: The Standing

FOREWORD

There are few words more powerful than *redemption*.

It speaks of restoration after ruin, beauty from ashes, and the kind of love that doesn't quit when things get messy. It is this rare kind of love: tough, tender, tested, and triumphant, that pulses through every chapter of *Grace Even After*.

This book is not a fairy tale. It is not a glossy highlight reel with curated captions. Instead, it is a deeply honest account of two people who chose to fight for each other when walking away may have seemed imminent. It is a story marked by betrayal, brokenness, and hidden battles, but also by divine grace, forgiveness, and the slow, sacred work of healing.

Through the pages that follow, you will meet a military kid and a small-town girl whose love was forged across distance and deep soul-searching. You will witness the painful unmasking of hidden struggles: shame, pornography, emotional exhaustion, and the courageous choice to bring darkness into light. You will walk through the valleys of distrust and heartbreak, and find hope in the gentle power of wise counsel, mentorship, and spiritual community.

But perhaps the most powerful theme of all is this: God still restores. He still heals. And when we surrender our broken pieces to Him, He rebuilds something even stronger.

If you have ever struggled in your marriage, doubted the possibility of restoration, or wondered whether grace can truly redeem the ugliest moments of your lives, this book is for you. With raw vulnerability and unwavering faith, the authors invite you to witness a miracle in motion: a marriage not just surviving, but *thriving* because of *Grace Even After.*

Let this book remind you that redemption is possible, that love is a daily choice, and that with Christ, no story is beyond rewriting.

Grace Even After is more than a testimony; it is a call to believe again.

Melvin Pillay
Motivational Speaker,
Christian Leadership Development Coach
& Business Growth Strategist

DEDICATION

This book is dedicated to our family, past and future. To our parents because of the foundation you laid for each of us; to our sisters for allowing us, firstborns, to make mistakes and errors, and our friends who caringly supported us from a distance along our journey thus far.

To our many friends and to those who walked alongside us, helped equip us, spoke words of encouragement, accepted us, loved us with agape love, and just gave your presence, thank you.

But above everything else, we dedicate this to our Heavenly Father Who knew us before we were born, Who destined us for His purpose, and has shown His immense grace and mercy towards His kids. His empowering through the Holy Spirit to initiate our journey to becoming battle tested, purified, refined, and sent out on our destiny He preordained for us.

ACKNOWLEDGEMENTS

We, Stephen and Krystina, are deeply grateful to those who have walked with us on this journey. This book is not just our work, it is a tapestry woven with the threads of friendship, mentorship, and encouragement from many remarkable people.

To Jack and April Tu, thank you for being more than friends; you have been our sounding board, prayer partners, and cheerleaders. Your unwavering belief in us, your laughter when we needed it most, and your quiet strength in moments of doubt gave us courage to keep going.

To John Bevere and the Bevere International team, your lives have been a living example of Kingdom purpose. Your boldness to speak truth with grace has been a constant inspiration. Thank you for reminding us that faith and excellence can walk hand in hand.

To Mark Gungor and Laugh Your Way Ministries, your ability to bring humor into the most challenging of topics has been a gift to us. Thank you for teaching us that joy and insight are powerful companions, and for cheering us on with such generosity of spirit.

To Bryan Mayer, LCSW – Coaching & Counseling, your wisdom and gentle guidance helped us navigate both personal growth and shared vision. Your thoughtful questions and professional insight brought depth to our journey that words can hardly capture.

To Melvin Pillay, we owe a special debt of gratitude. You didn't just believe in us, you challenged us, nudged us when we hesitated, and refused to let this dream remain only a dream. Thank you for connecting us to the right people and for opening the door to an editor and publisher who could see what we saw.

To Rose Ssali and the extraordinary team at Ssali Publishing House, thank you for taking our raw words and helping them shine. Your editorial care, creativity, and attention to detail gave this book its voice. You turned our thoughts into something beautiful, and your dedication was nothing short of inspiring.

Finally, to our families, friends, and every unseen hand that helped carry us here, thank you. Your encouragement, your prayers, and your belief in us have left fingerprints all over these pages. This book is as much yours as it is ours.

INTRODUCTION

There's a moment we will never forget.

It wasn't dramatic or loud. There were no grand declarations or tearful reconciliations. It was quiet, almost unremarkable to anyone else. Just the two of us, sitting on the couch, hands intertwined, our wedding rings catching the afternoon light. We were laughing, really laughing, for the first time in a long time. Not because everything was perfect, but because we realized we were *still here*. Still standing. Still choosing each other. Still being held together by a grace far greater than our efforts.

This book is our testimony.

It is not a manual from marriage experts. It's a raw, grace-laced offering from two people who have known pain, shame, and deep disappointment, but who have also come to know the Redeemer Who restores all things. We've journeyed through hidden struggles, trust broken and rebuilt, prayers whispered through tears, and long nights wondering if we'd make it.

And only by God's grace, we did.

We've now been married for over a decade, and if there's one truth we carry from our story, it is this: *Redemption is not only possible, it is God's heartbeat.* It doesn't erase the past, it rewrites it with purpose. It doesn't promise perfection, but it guarantees presence, *His presence.* And in the end, that's what made all the difference.

This book is written for the weary and the wondering. For the couple sitting in church, smiling on the outside, but breaking silently within. For the young couple full of hope and unaware of the storms ahead. For the counselor looking for language to hold space for someone else's pain. For the church leader seeking a culture of compassion over condemnation.

It's for anyone who dares to believe that God can breathe life into dry bones, heal fractured hearts, and make all things new.

We invite you to journey with us, not just through our story, but into the heartbeat of a Savior Who doesn't discard broken things. Instead, He redeems them.

Even after all we've been through, our hearts still sing. Imperfect. Incomplete. But held together by grace.

Still standing,

Krystina and Stephen Sterne, Jr.

Together in Love, Forgiveness, and Faith

PART I

LOVE IS A CHOICE

> "Every love story deserves a second chapter,
> if both hearts are willing to rewrite it.
>
> — *Unknown*

CHAPTER ONE

MILITARY KID MEETS SMALL TOWN GIRL

Stephen

By the time I turned eighteen, I had already seen more of the world than most people see in a lifetime. Spain, Turkey, Chile, and seemingly the whole wide world. My memories are stitched together with the scent of jet fuel and the shuffle of boots on concrete. I knew the art of packing up my life in cardboard boxes, how to memorize a new neighbourhood layout in under an hour, and how to make friends that you already knew you would lose in six months.

Being a military kid is like living everywhere and nowhere at once. I could tell you what the sun feels like in Madrid, Spain, how the call to prayer sounds at dusk in Adana, Turkey, or the way street vendors in Istanbul yell when you try to barter with them. I could describe those places better than I could tell you what my cousin's backyard looked like. That was my normal. Airports were familiar. New beginnings, routine.

But there was a cost. Every time we moved, I left something behind. A friend. A routine. A version of myself. I learned early on how to constantly adapt, how to keep a smile handy, and emotions tucked away. I became fluent in transition. Adaptation was my superpower, but hyper-independence became my shadow. Even now, I sometimes wonder what parts of me got left behind in all those moves.

And yet, I wouldn't trade it. There was a pride that came with being part of something bigger. My father wasn't just in the military, he lived it. Duty, discipline, and honor. That was the rhythm of our house. Morning prayers, the American flag, and a uniform properly prepared. Dad wasn't around much while serving in the U.S. Air Force, but he was always learning new things and sharing it with the family. My mother was always busy trying to make our military assignment feel like home, running the household, all while homeschooling my sister and me.

From them, I inherited more than just a love for country; I inherited a call to serve. Even as a kid, I wanted to, hopefully, one day wear a uniform. Not for glory, not to prove anything, but because I believed in what it stood for. God and country. Honor and purpose. I carried that in my bones.

Upon graduating high school, I knew I didn't want to go to college, because traditional schooling was not something I was interested in or believed I would excel at. Being homeschooled, I had already discovered that there is always a different way to view or approach things. Even as a young child, deposited deep into me was this natural and persistent perspective that the status quo wasn't the limit, but something to be challenged. I carried this chip on my shoulder that just because family, friends, and society said it had to be done a certain way, I wanted to break the mold and demonstrate that someone can obtain the same outcomes through different and non-traditional paths.

So not pursing college was the first step striking out on "becoming successful" by intentionally not pursuing higher education. I tried to join the military, and specifically wanted to pursue a career in special operations. I became aware that I had the ability to be calm and have clarity in chaos, so that seemed like a fit. But that door never did open, so I attempted to pursue a career in law enforcement. Over 25 applications processes and no acceptance, that never materialized either. But God had a plan, and again some unique doors were opened that allowed me to work for the U.S. Department of Defense.

Despite continuing to have some unique employment doors opened to me, I still had a very different and clear picture of how I wanted to live. I was never concerned about a defined career path, job titles, or social status. I knew what emotional distance felt like in a family and an environment of always presenting your polished version to the world. But I wanted deep, authentic, and genuine relationships; with my future wife, my future kids, and with all the people I'd meet along my life's journey. So I wasn't chasing job titles, income levels, and material things as specific achievements, but instead I want dearly to have relationships where it was safe to share, have disagreements without damage, and be an incubator of dreams, impact, and memories.

But for all I had seen, I was unprepared for what I would find in a quiet girl from a town with only a few traffic lights.

Krystina

I grew up in a small mountain town in California. Where everything we needed was just around the corner. The world I knew was a handful of streets, a church with a steeple you could see from anywhere in town, and our grocery store where we usually ran into someone we knew. It was safe, predictable, and wrapped in the kind of simplicity that makes it easy to take for granted.

Our neighbors didn't move away, they just got older. My sister and I were homeschooled, and excelled both as ballerinas and in equestrian sports. My best friend was my sister who shared a room with me. I always looked forward to the annual vacation to Hawaii or to visit family in Germany. And still, there was a quiet beauty in it all. A kind of sacred rhythm.

Even in all that goodness, my soul was still searching for something. My family loved each other, and my parents were dedicated to demanding careers in serving both the U.S. Air Force and our military. We enjoyed our evenings together eating delicious dinners my father prepared and spending time caring for our variety of pets.

We loved each other: however, spending time together was more rare than my childhood heart desired. I saw that being dedicated to a career could provide a great lifestyle, and yet I yearned for intimate relationships coupled with amazing memories.

Still yet, I craved something fuller. I wanted a love that reached the soul, a connection that stayed when things got messy and where joy lived regardless of life's happenings.

Then came Stephen.

Our parents introduced us. Nothing dramatic. Just one of those quiet setups that happens when two families cross paths and see something the kids don't yet. We were young. Curious. Polite. But something clicked.

He spoke with a calm confidence, like someone who had seen things. There was a steadiness to him, even in silence. I could tell he had lived more life than most and he wasn't trying to impress anyone, but he was a little rough around the edges. He listened more than he spoke, and when he did speak, there was thoughtfulness in his words. He was not good at small talk, but he made space for real talk.

Stephen

Krystina felt like peace and acceptance. That's the only way I can describe it. Her presence slowed me down. She wasn't trying to be anything. She just was. And I hadn't realized until I met her how much I needed that.

She didn't pepper me with questions about my life or my travels. She just let me unfold at my own pace. She didn't judge me for my past or my mistakes. I found myself talking about things I hadn't shared before; the places, the people, the goodbyes. And she didn't look at me like a novelty. She just listened.

There was a gentleness to her. A rootedness. Like she knew who she was and didn't feel the need to prove it. And that kind of confidence, especially in someone so young, disarmed me. It made me feel like maybe, finally, I had found a place to land.

Krystina

I had never met anyone like him. He talked about cities I had only read about in textbooks. He had eaten food I couldn't pronounce. And yet, he never made me feel small.

What struck me most was his ambition. He could've boasted, but he didn't. He spoke of his experiences like someone who had learned to see beauty and brokenness in equal measure. There was a tenderness under his strength, and something in his eyes told me he had carried pain he didn't speak of. He knew what he wanted and was chasing it, and it turns out it was a life that included marriage, adventure, and options.

I wanted to know him. Not just the stories. Him.

Stephen

We started with simple things: music, favorite foods, family quirks. But our conversations deepened quickly. We talked about being misunderstood. About what it felt like to belong, and what it felt like not to. I shared with her the sort of life I wanted to give to her, the lifestyle I had envisioned as a young teen for my future wife, and the sort of experiences and impact I wanted to make with my future bride.

Her steadiness anchored me. My stories stretched her. We didn't realize it then, but we were becoming home for each other.

Krystina

I think God brings people into our lives who carry the pieces we didn't know we were missing. Stephen had wings. I had roots. Together, we made something strong enough to hold both.

Looking back, I see now how our differences were never obstacles. They were invitations. We learned from each other, leaned into each other. We became more because we chose to see beyond what made us different.

We didn't know what was to come; the battles, the betrayals, the redemption. But in those early days, it was simple. Pure. Two hearts whispering *maybe*.

Stephen

I didn't know she'd be the one I'd walk through fire with. But I knew she was different. And for a kid who had lived a thousand lives, she made me want to stay in one. I loved like I had never felt before. I wasn't one who said "love" about hardly anything, because I felt that word deserved real depth and reverence. I heard people toss it around, but it appeared to me that when push came to shove, love vanished. But when someone like Krystina showed interest and acceptance of me as me, and gave me the space to share my struggles with my own mistakes, that reached deep inside of me to release love out of me.

Krystina

He didn't just come into my world. He expanded it. And I knew, even then, that my life would never be the same.

And so we were both military brats from opposite coasts that began a journey not written by chance, but carved by the quiet hand of Providence. A journey that would stretch us, test us, break us and ultimately remake us in the image of grace.

This was just the beginning.

CHAPTER TWO

LOVE ACROSS THE MILES

Krystina

Some love stories are written slowly—over coffee dates, Sunday walks, and lazy Saturday afternoons. Ours? Ours was actually while Stephen was working in the Middle East so it was written in pixels and pauses, across time zones, through digital sighs and unsent prayers. As Stephen prepared to travel overseas, I sensed something. It wasn't a dramatic spark or instant infatuation. It was quieter than that—like a whisper in my spirit. A gentle knowing.

We began with polite email check-ins. Little text updates. Friendly exchanges. But slowly, those turned into long emails, then nightly phone calls. I found myself waiting for the sound of his voice, the way his words came with intention. We had no shared restaurant, no favorite bench in the park, no inside jokes from long car rides. What we did have was trust. And time. And words.

He would speak so vulnerably about the loneliness of growing up on the move, always the new kid, always saying goodbye. I had never met anyone so honest about what they'd lost. And yet, he carried no bitterness. Just a kind of strength that wasn't showy or loud. It was there in how he listened. In how he remembered the small things I said.

It's strange how distance can sometimes bring you closer. Because we couldn't fall back on physical presence, we had to learn each other through conversation. We talked about childhood, fears, faith, even family dynamics. We commiserated that sharing emotions wasn't something we grew up with, and how I often felt a yearning for something deeper. He didn't judge. He didn't try to fix it. He just stayed present.

Of course, there were doubts. Days where I wondered if we were just imagining something that wouldn't work in real life. The time zones were a hassle. Silence between texts could stretch like an ache. But somehow, every time we talked, something inside me said, "Keep going."

And then he came to visit.

Stephen

I had always relied heavily on my gut instinct, and something was telling me that she could be "the one." And as with most things, I acted on my gut instinct quite fast by going to visit.

The California trip came at the perfect time, or maybe the worst. I was exhausted, unsure, and needing clarity. But mostly, I just wanted to see her. Not on a screen, not in my imagination. I needed to be where she lived, to walk the streets that shaped her, to sit across from her without buffering delays or dropped calls.

Her family welcomed me like I was already one of them. Her dad had that watchful calm, and her mom made me feel like I had always belonged. Krystina's world was nothing like mine. It was very routine. Predictable. And beautiful in its simplicity. I hadn't known how much I craved that until I saw her in it.

We took walks. Ran errands. Laughed with her sister. We weren't doing anything extraordinary. But every small moment felt sacred. It wasn't glamorous, it was real. And it grounded me in a way my years of travel never had.

I don't remember ever having any real insight into women, being that I grew up around a sometimes emotionally distant and very guarded mother, this woman was so alluring. The makeup, the smells, the soft skin, the freckles, the cutest laugh, those captivating blue eyes, and the taste of chap stick on her lips took me to a place in my spirit where I had never interacted with this softer, graceful, and incredibly beautiful womanhood. She was so different. She enjoyed holding hands, while I had to learn to accept and reciprocate that sort of simple physical touch because it often took me back to memories of physical touch that wounded me.

But, I was imagining a future with her. A real one. I wanted to ask her all the hard questions about faith, family, dreams. I wanted to map out the years ahead with her by my side.

But just when it felt like we were finding that rhythm, the call came.

Another unexplained door opened, and another very unique job opened up for me that demanded that I report—immediately. East Coast. No delay.

That night, I sat on the porch with her father. My heart beat loudly in my chest, not from fear, but from clarity. I did not know how to keep doing this long-distance thing. I didn't want more months of scattered calls and quick visits. I wanted her with me. I told him that.

He listened. Then looked me in the eye and said, "My daughter isn't going anywhere with you unless she's wearing your ring."

It wasn't said harshly. It was said with love. With protection. With honor.

And I respected him more for it.

Krystina

When Stephen proposed, it wasn't under fairy lights or some carefully orchestrated event. It was just us, at the airport of all places, hearts exposed. He looked at me with that same steady gaze he'd always given me, and asked the question that would change everything.

I said yes. Without hesitation.

Not because I knew what the future would look like. But because I knew who I wanted to walk into that future with. He wasn't promising perfection. He was promising presence. And for me, that was enough.

What followed was a whirlwind of a wedding. Modest. A local vineyard had only one Friday evening available. The caterer who had one remaining slot available. The florist was able to accommodate a simple yet beautiful display. There were a few rows filled with people who had known me since I was in pigtails. No real fancy décor, no Pinterest plans. Just vows. Just faith. Just love.

I wore a beautiful yet simple dress. He wore a suit that made him look like the man I had already known he was. When I walked down that aisle, I thought I was walking into a dream.

Stephen

She looked radiant.

I'd stood in ceremonies around the world, in chapels, in barracks, in parades. But that moment, watching her walk toward me, was the holiest ground I had ever stood on.

My vows weren't just words. They were confessions. I wasn't the guy with a neat past. But we were two lives with scars and stretch marks of the soul, saying, "Let's do this anyway."

I said, "For better, for worse..." not knowing how soon I'd taste both. Not knowing the unraveling that would come. Or the grace that would put us back together.

But I walked out with her, hand in hand. Rings glinting in the sun. Hearts wide open. And behind us, a community of witnesses. Ahead of us, only God knew.

Krystina

"Happily even after" isn't a promise you live—it's a choice you make. That day, we chose it. Chose each other. Chose love. We didn't need guarantees. We just needed grace.

And we had it.

CHAPTER THREE

HOMESICK HEART, SEARCHING SOUL

Krystina

Virginia was supposed to be a new beginning. A canvas upon which Stephen and I would paint our shared dreams. But beginnings often come wrapped in endings—of old comforts, old rhythms, and the places that once felt like home.

I left more than California behind when I boarded that plane eastward. I left sun-drenched sidewalks where everyone knew my name, neighbors who waved from porches they'd sat on since childhood, and a life so familiar it had become almost invisible in its comfort. But now, in this place of lush forests and humid summers, that absence roared louder than I'd anticipated.

Virginia was beautiful in its own right. The trees whispered ancient stories, the old brick buildings had character, and the people were polite enough. But polite was not the same as known. I missed the scent of lavender on cool evenings, missed my parent's kitchen table, missed walking down streets where every corner carried a memory.

Stephen

For me, I threw myself into work with the same discipline wired into me from childhood. From the outside, I was underqualified to be given the responsibility of facilitating engagements for the most senior representatives from around the globe in a very demanding and intense time of global conflict. I also couldn't talk about my work to Krystina, but I always strived to perform with excellence. And I brought those values to everything—especially our marriage. I came home every night with a smile, ready to hug Krystina tight and ask how her day had been.

But she wasn't thriving. I saw it in her eyes. The way her smile faded quickly. The way she retreated into quiet. The way the house felt too still, too sterile.

Krystina

The early days were the hardest. Living with Stephen's parents— kind as they were—made me feel like a guest in my own life. I tiptoed around the house, hesitant to make noise or take up space. They were warm and welcoming, but no amount of kindness could substitute for belonging. When we finally moved into our own home, I thought things might get better.

They didn't. At least not right away.

It wasn't the space; it was the silence. A silence that settled in my bones and made the walls feel too large, too echoing. There were days I didn't speak to anyone until Stephen came home. And even then, I filtered my words, afraid to sound ungrateful. How could I complain when I was loved so deeply? When he was trying so hard?

Still, love doesn't always silence the ache of dislocation.

One evening, after another long day of silence and self-doubt, I sat alone in our modest sun room. The sky had begun its soft descent into twilight. Crickets chirped in the distance. I rocked gently; in my hands, a half-folded dish towel lay forgotten. I stared into the quiet Virginia dusk, the air heavy with unfamiliar scents and the sound of cicadas humming like a foreign lullaby.

Under my breath, I hummed the haunting tune that had echoed in my mind all day:

> *"From a distance, the world looks blue and green...*
> *And the snow-capped mountains white..."*

It was the "from a distance" that pierced me most. My family, my friends, my sun-drenched California streets, they were all so far away. The laughter that once rang easily through my days now seemed to belong to another life. My beloved husband, though kind and devoted, was consumed by work. He came home weary, filled with deadlines, timelines, and things he couldn't even share with me.

I didn't want to burden him. After all, this was our dream, wasn't it? So I threw myself into housework. I baked. I cleaned. I reorganized closets I didn't even use. I ironed shirts he hadn't worn in weeks. I told myself I was building a home, but it still felt like someone else's.

Even our new home felt borrowed. Like I was walking through someone else's story in someone else's shoes.

My voice, fragile and aching, I didn't even realize I was crying.

Stephen

I had just returned from work, keys in hand, briefcase slung over my shoulder, when I saw her. She was rocking gently in the sun room with tear drenched cheeks. I stood still, just listening. Watching.

It hit me then, she was trying. God, she was trying so hard. But beneath that brave smile was a heart still rooted in California soil, still gasping for air, for home.

I walked into the sunroom slowly. She turned, startled, and immediately sat up straighter.

"I didn't hear you come in," she said.

"I know," I replied, kneeling beside her. "I heard you though."

She looked away embarrassed.

It was this moment that I realized just how hard and deeply painful this new life was for her.

Krystina

Tears filled my eyes. I hadn't meant for him to hear. I hadn't meant for him to know.

"I'm sorry," I whispered. "I don't mean to be difficult. I just... I miss home."

He pressed my hand to his chest.

"I know," he said. "And I've been so focused on building our future, I didn't realize you were mourning your past."

We sat there for a long while. No need for more words. The rocking chair creaked. The sky deepened to navy.

Stephen

Later that night, I looked up flights to California. I didn't tell her.

Because home isn't just a place, it's where you're seen, and heard, and understood. And sometimes, you have to travel miles to bring someone back to themselves.

Krystina

The next day, after my chores were done and the house fell quiet, I sat in the sun room again, tears silently tracing my cheeks. But in the quiet ache, a whisper rose in my spirit, a memory of stories I had once known.

Abraham. He too had been called away from the familiar:

> *"Leave your father's house and go to the land I will show you."*

He obeyed, walking in faith toward a promise yet unseen.

And then, there was Ruth, choosing to walk away from everything she knew, binding herself to Naomi with those immortal words:

> *"Where you go, I will go. Your people will be my people."*

It wasn't easy, but Ruth's obedience led her to a love story and to a legacy she couldn't have imagined. In doing so, she stepped into a lineage of redemption and kings.

Maybe I wasn't alone after all. Maybe this ache was part of the journey. Part of leaving one land to be planted in another. Perhaps the same God who guided Abraham, and who honored Ruth's courage, would meet me right here, in the quiet space between grief and grace.

CHAPTER FOUR

DISCOVERING THE HIDDEN BATTLE (PORNOGRAPHY AND SHAME)

Krystina

I hadn't noticed the signs at first. Life had finally begun to feel like it was falling into place, at least from the outside. Our new home brought me a measure of peace, and though the ache of homesickness still lingered like a low fog, I was learning to smile. But there was something off. Something in Stephen's eyes that didn't quite meet mine. A distance. A shadow.

The truth didn't come with a crash, but with a whisper; an accidental glimpse of his browser history. My heart dropped, ice flooding my veins as the images blinked across the screen. Denial rose swiftly. Maybe it's a pop-up. A mistake. But the reality settled like lead in my stomach. This wasn't a mistake. It was a pattern.

I addressed this with him, and Stephen's confession came with tears, shame, and the hollow sound of something inside me breaking.

"I've struggled with this for years," he whispered. "Since I was a teenager."

He explained that his exposure began early, far earlier than any child should encounter such things. A trusted adult had left pornographic websites open, as if they were no more dangerous than comic books. The free and easy to access material, that started with curiosity, turned into chains. And over time, those chains became familiar, binding, yes, but strangely comforting in a world that often felt cold and disconnected.

For a boy who grew up with isolation as a constant companion, this hidden coping mechanism had become both an escape and a prison. And while he tried, truly tried, to leave it behind, it had sunk deep roots into the soil of his mind.

I reeled. How could this be the man I loved? The man who held my hand when we prayed at night?

My first reaction was betrayal. Not just because he had kept a secret, but because this secret felt like a stranger had entered our bed, our sacred space. Shame echoed through our home like thunder in a canyon.

He apologized, again and again. Promised change. Swore he would seek help. And sometimes, it seemed he was winning. But then would come the fall. Again. And again.

I began to question everything. Was love enough? Was forgiveness even possible?

In the quiet of my confusion, I turned to the One Who never turns away from broken people.

One morning, my Bible fell open to the story of King David, not just the slayer of giants, but the broken man who fell into lust and deception, betraying God, his people, and a woman's dignity. And yet, David wasn't discarded. He was rebuked, but also restored. Psalm 51 became my lifeline:

> *"Create in me a clean heart, O God, and renew a right spirit within me."*

If God could redeem David, could He not redeem Stephen?

Another story surfaced: the prophet Hosea, told by God to marry a woman who would be unfaithful, as a living parable of God's relentless love for wayward people. I wept when I read it. Hosea kept loving Gomer, not because she deserved it, but because God's love never gave up.

And then there was the woman caught in adultery. Ready to be stoned by the crowd until Jesus knelt beside her and said,

> *"Let he who is without sin cast the first stone."*

Instead of condemnation, He offered restoration.

These stories didn't excuse Stephen's behavior. But they framed it in the language of grace, a grace that confronts, convicts, and calls for repentance, but never gives up on the hope of healing.

Stephen was also beginning to see his inner struggle for what it was: not a bad habit, but a form of bondage. He sought professional help and began therapy.

But recovery isn't linear. Setbacks and the loud voice of shame accusing him of being beyond saving. But he clung to the words of 2 Corinthians 12:9:

> "My grace is sufficient for you, for My strength is made perfect in weakness."

Our marriage felt like a battlefield. At times, bruised and raw. At others, filled with glimmers of hope. We had to learn new ways of communicating—of being honest without cruelty, of holding space for pain while still believing in healing.

There were moments I wanted to walk away. Not because I hated him, but because I didn't know how to hold the weight of it all. And yet, each time, something held me back: a quiet voice, a nudge from the Holy Spirit, a reminder that true love is tested not at the altar, but in the fire.

Stephen, often tearful, confessed how unworthy he felt. And through gritted faith, I chose to believe that this man, this broken man, was still worth fighting for.

I remember telling him one night, through tears of my own, "I didn't say 'I do' to a perfect man. I said it to you. And I still believe in who you can become."

Stephen

I remember it clearly as day when my secret was discovered. A careless mistake of leaving a device with adult material around our home.

As soon as she discovered it, the most tense, awkward, and soul tearing response was on display.

She could barely speak, ask any questions, or spew the anger, hurt, and betrayal she felt inside.

But I knew it, I had done the unthinkable. I never intended for my behaviour to so deeply and radically hurt the only person I had ever really loved and was the biggest blessing I had ever received. A woman who loved me and accepted me, but that was now weighing in the balance.

As a kid, I knew pornography was wrong. I had heard people say that, heard pastors and Sunday school teachers say it was wrong, but it became an activity that despite knowing the wrongness, I hadn't yet experienced the consequences.

There's no way to calculate the exact amount of porn online. But experts estimate 4% of all global Internet traffic is pornography. Statistics report the following:

- 61% of the general population report viewing pornography.
- 78% of men watch pornography.
- 44% of women watch pornography.
- 12 is the average age of first exposure.
- 54% of practicing Christians watch pornography.
- 75% of practicing Christian men watch pornography.
- 40% of practicing Christian women consume pornography.
- 22% of practicing Christians view pornography at least once a week.

Before marriage, it was a personal activity that seemed harmless. No one knew, there was no sex before marriage, no pregnancy, and it seemed to have little to no impact in my life.

But that just changed. BIG TIME.

I panicked after being caught the first time. I thought marriage would make the desire go away, I thought that being able to have a sexual partner would change things, and I didn't think the ramifications of that behaviour would turn an already challenging new marriage into a bonfire.

I tried to apologize, say that I didn't mean to hurt her. That I hadn't already lost interest or sexual attraction to my absolutely beautiful wife. But the pain point of any addiction or self-destructive behaviour stems from wounds. But I was completely blind to my past wounds, so I figured time would heal things.

And it happened again, caught red handed. What do I do? I can't seem to shake this habit, but I also can't stand the idea that my wife would leave me over a website.

I apologized again, and again, and again. Trust was obliterated. Excuses were rampant from me. I was stuck in a chasm between a wife who I hurt beyond my wildest imagination and a seemingly innocuous sin that I couldn't seem to overcome.

And shame was the coat I wore every day. Why did I have to develop this behaviour? Why did my wife happen to find out? Why did no one tell me that this would happen?

I never wanted to continue, nor did I tell myself it was acceptable. The part of my DNA that just had to say no to the status quo rose up. Was I going to be a victim or a victor? Was I going to say to my wife that my habit won over our marriage? Was I just going to add to the 55%+ divorce rate in the church?

No, I had seen too many men abdicate, destroy, or allow their marriage to implode by playing the victim.

So I made a decision.

I was going to win the battle over my secret, and win the war of our crumbling marriage.

I had to get help, any way possible.

Our story is still being written. It's not tied with a pretty bow. But it is a story of courage, of confession, and of hard-won healing.

As we share it now, we do so not as a perfect couple, but as two people daring to tell the truth for the sake of others who sit silently in shame, afraid their struggle is too dark to speak aloud.

My shame did not define me. Krystina's pain did not destroy her.

And our marriage, scarred though it may be, became a canvas for grace, a place where redemption is not just a distant hope, but a lived reality.

PART II

THE WRESTLING

CHAPTER FIVE

THE CHURCH — A SANCTUARY FOR THE BROKEN OR A COURTROOM FOR THE CONDEMNED?

Krystina

There was a time I truly believed the church was the one place where healing would be inevitable. I wanted to believe that if I collapsed anywhere, it could be in the house of God. But when Stephen's battle came to light and my pain became raw, our years of being involved in the local church didn't feel like refuge. It appeared to be more like a courtroom.

Over the years in church I had experienced and heard whispers amongst fellow believers who had made mistakes. Silent stares. Well-meaning, but poorly timed Scriptures spoken more like verdicts than lifelines. Unsolicited advice. And a quiet pressure, to separate, to move on, to keep quiet so no one would "taint" the image of a godly life.

I wasn't looking for applause. I was desperate for help. I didn't need people to excuse sin. I longed for compassion. For someone to look me in the eye and say, "We're staying with you." But instead, the loudest sound was judgement. No one offered to sit with us. No one said, "We've been there too."

So I asked a question that lingered:

Is the church truly a hospital for the broken, or a courtroom for the condemned?

Stephen

In my years in the church, I noticed there is often an unspoken expectation in church culture: that everyone should look tidy. That testimonies should be shared after the mess is over, if ever. That pain, addiction, and marital failure belong in whispered side conversations or behind closed counselling doors, not in the open, and not at the altar. When a topic like pornography was whispered, the topic was dismissed and moved past as quickly as possible. So here I was, looking for help while I was seemingly destroying a marriage that I wanted to save, with no help to be found.

I discovered that statistics show:

- 67% of pastors have a personal history with porn.
- 18% of pastors in the United States currently struggle with pornography.

- Only 7% of pastors report their church has a ministry program for those struggling with porn.

"A study at a Christian university found that among Christian students who use pornography, 43 percent of men and 20 percent of women say their pornography use worsened their relationship with Christ. Further, 20 percent of men and 9 percent of women reported their pornography use caused them to lose interest in spiritual things."

So I turned back to Scripture, because if God's Word didn't still speak to people like us, then what were we even doing?

Krystina

And it did speak. Loud and clear. I saw myself in Rahab. The outsider. The woman with a stained past. But God didn't just save her, He elevated her. Welcomed her into the lineage of Christ. Where others saw a label, God saw faith.

Stephen

For me, it was Paul. Saul, really. A man whose name once struck fear. Who persecuted the very people he'd one day pastor. When God turned his life around, even the early church struggled to accept it. It took one man, Barnabas, to stand beside him. To vouch for the grace of God at work. That simple act of solidarity opened the door for Paul's ministry. I often wondered, where was our Barnabas?

Krystina

And then there was Hagar. Used. Discarded. Alone in the wilderness. And God finds her. Not a prophet. Not a priest. God Himself. She's the first to give God a name in Scripture—*El Roi*, the God who sees me. God sees. Even when others turn away.

None of these people were polished. They were messy. Complicated. But God didn't erase their stories, He redeemed them. That's the pattern of Scripture: God working through weakness, not despite it.

Stephen

So I asked: if God works through broken people, why are churches so scared of brokenness? Why is it generally just attend and pretend to cover any cracks from showing? There were those who judged without understanding. Who offered clichés when presence was needed. Who said things like "just pray more" or "at least you're still together," not realizing those words felt more like wounds than help. There were those who avoided eye contact, who kept their distance once they found out. Maybe we've confused holiness with appearance. Maybe we've forgotten that righteousness is a gift, not a trophy. Maybe the church has forgotten its mission to help those in need, not create a life behind a façade. Because if a church isn't a place to go for help, for counsel, and for equipping, then it's merely a community of people pretending that life is "good."

Krystina

I cried over the church. Not because I hated it, but because I loved it. I still believe in it. But I also believe we need to make room again for messy grace. The kind of grace that can sit with someone in pain without needing to fix it or broadcast it.

Stephen

I wanted to be seen for what I was—a man who had failed, yes—but also a man desiring for guidance in the process of becoming new. I didn't need pity. I needed the kind of accountability that doesn't come with shame. The kind of truth that heals rather than humiliates.

Eventually, we found a community like that. It wasn't a stuffy church with a tall steeple, suit coats, and activities each evening. It was a gathering of flawed people sharing their real stories. A pastor who had scars of his own and didn't hide them. Here, testimonies weren't about spiritual perfection, they were about redemption. Confession wasn't met with silence. It was met with tears, prayer, and actual help.

Krystina

That community reminded us of Jesus' words:

> *"It's not the healthy who need a doctor, but the sick."*

We had to admit our sickness. Our need. Our ache. And instead of being turned away, we were embraced.

Stephen

The early church wasn't perfect. But it was personal. People met in homes. Broke bread. Confessed sins. Carried burdens. That's the kind of church we believe in. One where the cross, not control, leads the way.

Krystina

We still believe in the church. But we believe she needs to return to her first love, to the heart of Christ. To be more like the father running toward the prodigal, and less like the older brother peering out the window in judgment.

I remember the woman caught in adultery. Dragged out, exposed, humiliated. She expected condemnation. But Jesus knelt in the dirt beside her. He disarmed the crowd. And then He turned to her with tenderness:

> *"Neither do I condemn you. Go, and sin no more."*

That's the balance—grace and truth. One without the other is incomplete.

Stephen

This story isn't about making peace with sin. It's about fighting for restoration. For the kind of redemption that happens when we walk people home, not throw them out.

People like a pastor who pulled me aside and said, "You are not disqualified." Or a couple who invited us over for dinner, not to fix us, but just to be with us. These types of people became actual ministers of quiet mercy. They didn't need to understand everything. They just chose to walk with us.

Just like Jesus, who dined with the shamed. Who wrote in the dust beside the accused. Who reached out to touch the unclean. Who looked past performance and saw the heart. He was never afraid of the mess. He sat in it, healed in it, and redeemed through it.

Krystina

The church can be a courtroom. Or it can be a hospital. We get to choose what kind of community we create; because in the end, we're all broken. Some of us just know how to hide it better. But God sees. And still, He calls. Still, He covers.

As I've often said:

"The real scandal is not our sin. It's that grace would dare to cover it."

Stephen

And maybe that's the greatest miracle of all—not that the church is perfect, but that it's the one place on earth where sinners become saints. Not by merit. But by mercy.

But the church we experienced didn't seem to echo that Gospel. The Gospel we believed in was full of second chances. It was about mercy triumphing over judgment. About Jesus Who stooped low enough to write in the dust, Who didn't throw the first stone, Who offered forgiveness even as He hung on a cross.

We hope the church, not just the corporate church, will become a place where people don't need to pretend. Where pain isn't exploited. Where marriages can be rebuilt without shame. And where judgement is exchanged for agape love.

CHAPTER SIX

MENTORS, SAFE SPACES AND WISE COUNSEL

There is a sacred strength in reaching out. And there is divine wisdom in knowing whom to reach for.

Krystina

After the shock of discovering Stephen's hidden secret, when everything sacred felt broken and the air between us thick with pain and unspoken words, we stood at a crossroads. Alone, we were unravelling. Was that it? Was this the end? Was this how our love story was going to end, shattering my heart into a million little fragments? Was there any hope or help for us to be able to stitch the pieces back together?

I spoke with a chaplain once, while I was in the midst of denying this whole reality. I viewed vulnerability as a weakness, so I was trying to carry this whole burden alone.

During our conversation, he shared with me God already knew that I was so angry at Him and felt betrayed by the husband that He gave me. This simple comment seared my soul, as it was this revelation that led me to shift from denying and running from my pain, to the acceptance of looking past myself to Stephen. This was not a man trying to hurt me, but a wounded boy trying to fix himself.

It started with a conversation neither of us wanted to have.

"We should talk to someone," Stephen's voice barely audible over the cry and ache of my broken heart.

I thought about the conversation with the chaplain, but he was on the other side of the country. We had a few people who were safe places to share, but they could not help. We needed someone who was a safe place, who knew it was possible for restoration, and could give us practical counsel on how to do it.

We were both wary. We had heard the stories—gossip disguised as prayer requests, well-meaning advice laced with spiritual pride, friends who took sides instead of standing in the gap. We needed wisdom, not just sympathy. Truth, not judgment. People who could hold our secrets without crushing us under religious expectations.

We took a leap and met with a counsellor who was able to provide a safe place, whose journey also navigated restoration, and was able to equip us with some very practical measures we could apply for day-to-day application. But there was a layer deeper that needed exposure to provide healing.

Shortly after, David and Hope were similar ages, wise through their own journey, and had been fully restored by God's grace. In our very first meeting, the woman spoke gently about "being broken, but beloved." The husband, quiet and steady, had a way of seeing people without overwhelming them.

"Let's call them," Stephen said.

It's critical to know that there are two categories of people when you are looking for help, counselling, or a safe place. First, there are those who care, but cannot actually help. Unfortunately, for most of us those are most commonly our close family and friends. They care and want the best for you, but you need someone who has been and seen where you are. And most importantly, someone who has been battle tested and conquered the same season you are experiencing.

A Conversation That Held No Condemnation

When we first met David and Hope in person, Stephen expected a sermon. I braced for the sting of pity. But what we received was a conversation full of peace and hearts full of understanding.

We shared everything. The fear. The failure. The pain.

And the couple listened—truly listened. No gasps. No interruptions. Just nods, soft sighs, and eyes that said, we've been there too, in our own way.

"You are not your worst moments," David said quietly. "You're more than the sin you fell into and more than the pain that found you."

They spoke of grace. Of battle scars. Of how sin thrives in secrecy and shame, but weakens in the light of truth and community. The couple didn't pretend to have magic answers. But they had presence—and presence was enough.

Hope leaned forward and looked at me with eyes that mothered my spirit. "You're not crazy for hurting. You're undoubtedly courageous for staying."

Tears flowed. Healing began.

The Power of Godly Counsel

It wasn't just emotional relief. It was deeply spiritual. What was happening that evening was more than therapy—it was koinonia, the kind of fellowship Scripture celebrates. The kind that sharpens, shelters, and strengthens.

Scripture echoes this wisdom time and again:

• Jethro advised Moses to delegate and rest, offering practical, godly insight that preserved Moses from burnout and collapse (Exodus 18).

• Nathan confronted David—not with cruelty but with courageous truth wrapped in relationship (2 Samuel 12).

• Elizabeth, filled with the Holy Spirit, became the safe space for Mary, the unwed teenage mother carrying the Savior of the world (Luke 1:39–45). Mary didn't go to a temple first, she ran to someone who could hold her story without dropping her.

Each of these figures provided something vital—spiritual maturity, compassion, perspective, and grace.

That night, we realized: community is not just about company. It's about discernment. Not everyone should know your story, but someone must. The right someone.

Safe Spaces Aren't Perfect Spaces

We began praying before conversations: "Lord, lead us to the people who carry Your heart."

And God did.

Through mentorship and community, we saw our wounds reflected in others who had healed. We heard stories of infidelity forgiven.

Of depression overcome. Of marriages that looked like ashes, but became altars.

These weren't polished people. They were simply present, prayerful, and patient.

The Wisdom to Speak, and the Grace to Be Still

Sometimes, it wasn't even the advice that mattered. It was the reminder: you are not alone.

One woman simply held my hand and said, "We'll sit with you in the dark until the light returns."

Stephen, meanwhile, found accountability, not the kind that shamed him into guilt, but the kind that called him higher. A friend who met with him every week, asked hard questions, and reminded him of who he was in Christ. Not a slave to lust. Not a statistic. A son.

Healing Happens in Relationships

I often thought back to Ruth. That young widow didn't have to follow Naomi, but she did. And in doing so, she stepped into her destiny. Relationships guided her into restoration. Had she stayed behind in Moab, her story may have ended in sorrow. But companionship re-routed her future.

Or Elisha, who left everything to follow Elijah, not for fame but to serve and to learn (1 Kings 19:19–21).

Or even the disciples. Jesus could've chosen to disciple each of them separately, but He placed them in a group. A messy, opinionated, sometimes irritating group. Because growth rarely happens in isolation.

What We Learned

We learned:

- It's okay to need help.
- It's essential to be selective.
- It's life-giving to be surrounded by people who love God and understand humanity.

We also learned that healing doesn't always come from hearing "it will be okay"—sometimes, it comes from hearing, "I've been there too, and I'm still standing."

In our most vulnerable season, what saved us wasn't perfection—it was presence.

CHAPTER SEVEN

PRESENCE

Stephen

In our most vulnerable season, what saved us wasn't perfection, it was presence. Not the kind that demanded answers or rushed to fix the broken pieces, but the kind that quietly sat with us in the middle of the storm. It was the presence of those who listened without judgment, the mentors who had been down the long road of disappointment and healing and could say, "You're not alone." It was the presence of godly friends who carried our burden in prayer, and most of all, the gentle, unwavering presence of God, who did not flinch at our brokenness nor withdraw in our shame.

When the ground beneath our feet shifted, when decisions were heavy and our hearts were fragile, wisdom became a lifeline. But not all voices could be trusted, and not every listening ear was safe. I soon learned that while it was vital to talk to someone, it was equally critical that the person, or people, I turned to were mature in spirit, seasoned in grace, and rooted in truth.

Krystina

We found with mentors that we'll call David and Hope, our age, a similar broken to restored journey, and having grown deep roots anchored in God. In our darkest hour, what held us together wasn't answers; it was their sacred presence. They didn't try to fix us. They didn't offer neatly packaged advice. They simply stayed. They knew how to sit in silence and hold space without judgment.

That kind of presence reminded me of Jesus in the boat during a violent storm. He didn't prevent the storm, but He calmed it from within—and that steadied the disciples (Mark 4:35–41). I didn't need every wave of uncertainty to cease. I just needed to know that we weren't alone in the storm.

Naomi's presence in Ruth's life came to mind too. She didn't just instruct, she walked beside. She shaped Ruth's choices with quiet resilience and spiritual depth. Ruth's life took an unexpected turn toward blessing because Naomi didn't run from pain, but walked faithfully through it.

Stephen

And I thought of Aaron and Hur—silent yet strong—holding up Moses' arms when he was too weary to carry the weight of leadership and battle (Exodus 17:12). They didn't need the spotlight. Their strength was in support, in lifting when someone else was falling. That image struck me deeply because in moments when I was too broken to stand, our mentors carried us in prayer. Not loudly, not publicly, just faithfully.

Krystina

And when my own arms felt heavy, when the betrayal made it hard to breathe, I found myself recalling that image too. A prayer whispered by our mentor couple was enough to lift me, to let me breathe again.

But more than anything, it was the presence of the Divine in fiery trials that comforted us. Just as Shadrach, Meshach, and Abednego stood in the flames, not alone but with a fourth figure Whose presence defied explanation (Daniel 3:25), we had moments when shame and fear threatened to consume us. But God met us there invisibly, but unmistakably.

And I think often of Peter. After his failure, when he returned to the place where he had once known purpose, it wasn't a lecture that met him. It was breakfast on the shore and a quiet invitation to try again (John 21). Jesus didn't demand explanations. He simply stayed. He restored with presence.

Stephen

Another couple who walked with us didn't try to fix us. They listened with eyes full of mercy. They prayed without fanfare. They reminded us, wordlessly at times, that even in the mess, God still draws near.

Safe spaces matter. Wise counsel matters. But above all, presence matters. Because sometimes, the most sacred thing you can offer another human being is the ministry of not walking away.

CHAPTER EIGHT

GUARDING EACH OTHER'S VULNERABILITY

Stephen

Every heart carries fragile places. For me, the journey to rebuild demanded more than honesty, it also demands a holy tenderness. Vulnerability was a new destination for me, but where we both discovered true intimacy for the first time. I started to peel back the deepest layers of my soul to my soulmate, and that full exposure is the battleground for a marriage to become battle tested. Most of us like the benefits and rewards of marriage, but very few of us men have the guts and courage to push into pain, uncover our wounds, and curiously explore vulnerability with ourselves.

I had always dreamed and expected of myself that I would be an upstanding husband, present father, and someone who would break away from the generational curses of lust, immorality, and infidelity. And having been forced to face the hidden beast, there was a decision to be made.

Was I going to let excuses and self-deception lead my marriage? Or was I going to own up to my wounds, thoughts, and behaviour?

In those early days of rebuilding, one truth kept returning to me: I was solely responsible for nearly destroying our marriage, and it was going to take everything I had and more to rebuild it. It is said that time heals all wounds, but that is in fact not true at all. Time passing does not restore, rebuild, or rehabilitate a marriage. Nor do wounds heal in environments of judgment and shame. My healing process actually began with confrontation, because whatever is tolerated is also endorsed. Along with confrontation, a decision response is required; accept ownership on a path to pursue healing and restoration or just throw in the towel and quit. After being confronted, it forced me to expose my vulnerabilities that were shared in small sanctuaries of safety. I needed wise counsel, accountability, but most of all a significant amount of rewiring who I believed I was. Who was I in my own eyes? How did my Heavenly Father see me? And could I ever change how Krystina saw me?

At this point of reflection, the looming question was *who was I going to be?* Would I let the voice of defeat triumph, or would I peel back my wounds and allow His light to expose the darkness?

I actually began to pray, not just for restoration, but for the wisdom to be gentle with her. To realize that she would lay out my course for restoring our trust. I did not nor should I get to make any demands or expectations based on just being in a marriage or being the husband. Counsel and prayer became my lifeline. In prayer, I only needed to have a childlike conversation of my fears and failures to God, and gradually, to Krystina. I saw how often I had spoken truth without love, or held back love in the name of truth. And I repented, not only for what I had done, but for how little I had known how to love her well.

Krystina

For me, the journey was about learning to soften without shattering. I remembered the story of Adam and Eve. When they sinned and realized they were naked, shame entered the world. Their instinct was to hide. But God came walking in the garden, not to destroy them, but to find them. Even in their failure, He made garments to cover them. Even when we fall, God covers us.

I held onto that truth as we began to rebuild trust. I had to let go of the need to defend myself and instead seek to understand. I had to create space where Stephen could be vulnerable again; where he could be weak without fear of being wounded further.

I set new boundaries, not to wall each other out, but to protect what we were building. I began to say things like, "I need space right now, but I'm not withdrawing my love," and he learned to respond, "Can we revisit this later? I want to give you the response you deserve."

Our communication changed. It became less about proving points and more about sharing hearts. We replaced accusations with questions, assumptions with clarity. Small acts of care—like a handwritten note, a warm embrace after a hard conversation—became the building blocks of new trust.

Stephen

I started to turn to Scripture for guidance. Peter wrote that love covers a multitude of sins. And I saw it in Jesus. He didn't shame the woman at the well. He saw her. He didn't condemn the woman caught in adultery. He knelt beside her in the dirt. I needed a father who saw me for who I was destined to be, and not for the wake of destruction that I was trying to clean up.

I started cultivating this kind of presence at home. I remember hearing that someone with my personality type needed to become very accustomed to apologizing and repentance. When tension rose, I had to pause to breathe. I remembered the sacredness of actually being blessed with a wife who loved me enough to call out my behaviour. I stopped keeping score. Instead I started thinking "How can I guard her heart today?"

There were still lots of missteps. Defensiveness returned at times. But I kept returning to counsel, prayer, to Scripture, to each other. I learned to say, "I'm sorry," and "I forgive you," a lot, with no strings attached.

Krystina

And the fruit of that started to show. There was laughter again, unguarded and free. There were deep conversations. Long walks. The distance between us shortened. One morning, with sunlight streaming into our room, I whispered, "I'm starting to feel safe again."

It wasn't a declaration of perfection. It was a recognition of presence. I was beginning to feel safe, not because the pain had disappeared, but because Stephen had started to treasure my heart.

Guarding each other's vulnerability meant being shields. Standing between our beloved and the voices of accusation even when those voices lived in our own minds. Saying, "I see your wounds, and I will not use them against you."

It also meant being honest about our own weaknesses. Stephen shared how afraid he'd been of not measuring up. I admitted the walls I'd built to avoid pain. And in those moments, we didn't recoil, we leaned in.

Stephen

Christ-like love isn't afraid of the naked soul. It covers without controlling. Protects without possessing. It mirrors the love of God Who, even when we were still sinners, drew near.

Krystina

Our home started to become a sanctuary for the first time ever. Not perfect. But protected. A place where failure wasn't fatal. A place where confession opened doors to grace. A place where truth walked hand in hand with tenderness.

In a world that exploits vulnerability, we chose to be different. We chose Christ.

And in choosing Him, we found not just healing, but holiness.

In my quiet moments, I found that writing down my concerns, questions, and fears, and seeking the guidance of the Holy Spirit, helped put things into perspective like nothing else had done.

PART III

THE HEALING BEGINS

CHAPTER NINE

GRACE GREATER THAN OUR SIN

Stephen

There is a kind of grace that reaches into the darkest corners of your life. The kind that finds you where shame lives. Where failure echoes. Where hiding feels safer than healing. I know because I have been there. We both have. And what we found was not cheap grace, but grace that cost something. Grace that came slowly. Grace that stayed.

For me, this destructive habit was a thief. It took things I did not know I would miss until they were gone. It robbed me of time, of dignity, of the trust others had in me, and worst of all, it tried to steal love. It lied constantly. It told me shame was forever and that I would never be anything more than my worst moment. There was nothing quick about recovery. It was being delivered through the power of the Holy Spirit and His grace empowering me that became the lifeline pulling me through from the storm.

God's grace did not excuse my sin, but it overcame it. The words of Romans 5:20 became more than Scripture to me. They became personal:

"Where sin increased, grace abounded all the more."

That is what I found when I stopped running. Not a Judge waiting to condemn me, but a Father waiting to restore me. He did not ignore the mess. But He did invite me to come home.

The Grace That Carried Us

Krystina was not just watching from the sidelines. She was in the middle of the storm too. A prayer warrior when I had no words. An intercessor when I could not find the strength to stand. And sometimes, just a broken-hearted wife trying to cling to promises when nothing made sense. She could have walked away. And at times, maybe she wanted to. But she stayed. Not because it was easy, but because she believed in something stronger than feelings. She chose to hope.

Her love became a vessel for God's grace. Not perfect, not without struggle, but rooted in covenant. Watered in prayer. Grown through pain.

It took time to rebuild trust. It took time to believe again. There were long conversations. Counseling sessions. And above all, a surrender to the fact that healing would not come through effort alone, but through grace. I had to become the person I was destined to be. And that meant being honest about who I had become.

Our marriage could have died. But it didn't. Because God is still in the business of resurrection.

The Lie We Had to Confront

Have you ever wondered if your sin was too great to be forgiven? That your story was too far gone? That the wounds were too deep to heal?

Those are lies that too many people believe, and we believed that for a while. But God told us something else.

We did not just stay married. We found true joy. We didn't just get through it. We learned to thrive. Our story is not "happily ever after." It is "happily even after." Even after failure. Even after betrayal. Even after we thought it was over, because grace did not give up on us.

The Long Road of Forgiveness

Healing does not come without forgiveness. And forgiveness can be one of the hardest things you will ever choose.

I had to forgive the person who opened the door into addiction for me, whether carelessly or deliberately. That moment from my childhood grew into confusion, into shame, into secrets. Forgiving them was not saying it did not matter. It was saying it would no longer define me. It was taking back the power from a memory that had haunted me for years.

But even harder was forgiving myself. It is one thing to ask God for mercy. It is another to give it to yourself. I had to stare down regret and shame and say, "You do not get to hold me anymore." Grace met me in that valley. Not just with comfort, but with truth. That I am not what I have done. That God's promises are for me too. That I am not disqualified.

Her Forgiveness

Krystina had her own road of forgiveness. She had to forgive me—yes. But also herself. For the moments she turned away instead of toward. For the times she stopped praying. For the days when she thought about running. For the guilt that whispered, "If you had more faith, maybe this wouldn't have happened."

Grace met her too. Not to shame her, but to hold her. Not to demand more, but to remind her that she never carried this burden alone.

The Cross in the Middle

What kind of grace is this? That forgives both the one who failed and the one who was hurt? That covers the one who caused the wound and the one who is still bleeding? Only the grace that comes from the cross.

It forgives. But it also redeems.

Forgiveness says, "You are no longer guilty."
Redemption says, "You are still chosen."

Forgiveness says, "You may leave your past."
Redemption says, "You have a future."

Forgiveness breaks the chains.
Redemption teaches you to walk free.

We didn't stop at forgiveness. We stepped into redemption. And in doing so, we found purpose in our pain. Our scars became stories. Our love became not just something we rescued, but something strong enough to help others. A new kind of love.

Grace in the Ordinary

Forgiveness, for us, was not a ceremony. It wasn't a big moment with fireworks and closure. It was quiet. Daily. Lived. It looked like sitting together when there was nothing to say. Holding hands again even when it felt unfamiliar. Choosing to stay kind. Choosing to see each other not as we had been, but as we were becoming.

We prayed together. Sometimes through tears. Sometimes in silence. But we stayed. We loved. Even when it hurt.

Sometimes forgiveness looked like reaching across the bed at midnight just to whisper, "I'm still here." Sometimes it was washing dishes side by side. Or crying in the car, and not needing to explain why.

Forgiveness was not an event. It became our rhythm.

Choosing to Stay

For her, staying was not weakness. It was strength refined by fire. It was choosing grace over memory. Mercy over resentment. She prayed when she had no words. She stayed when she could have walked away. And she never stopped believing that God could redeem even this.

For me, it meant no more hiding. No more pretending. It meant facing the truth. But also learning how to let someone love me— even when I felt I didn't deserve it. Accepting her forgiveness. Not sabotaging the second chance. Believing I was not a lost cause.

We both learned that forgiveness is not forgetting. It is remembering without reliving. It is building something new on broken ground. It is resurrection in real time.

Broken, Blessed, Shared

There are still no guarantees in life. But there is grace. And it is enough.

Forgiveness is now our daily bread. Broken. Blessed. Shared. We keep offering it to each other. We keep receiving and accepting it from God.

We are living proof that grace is greater than sin. That mercy triumphs over judgment. That love, real love, does not walk away when the storm hits. It anchors in.

Our story is still being written. It's not tied with a pretty bow. But it is a story of courage, of confession, and of hard-won healing. Not a story of perfect people. But of a perfect Savior who met us in our imperfection and said, "You are forgiven. Go and sin no more."

As we share it now, we do so not as a perfect couple, but as two people daring to tell the truth—for the sake of others who sit silently in shame, afraid their struggle is too dark to speak aloud.

My failures did not define me.

Krystina's pain did not destroy her.

And our marriage, scarred though it may be, became a canvas for grace—a place where redemption is not just a distant hope, but a lived reality.

We are still going. Still growing. Still forgiving. And still, by grace, together.

CHAPTER TEN

YOU ARE FORGIVEN... GO AND SIN NO MORE

Krystina

I often return in my mind to those words: *You are forgiven... Go and sin no more.* Not as a cold command, but as a healing, lifting truth. A hand stretched out toward the ground where I had fallen. For both Stephen and me, those words were more than a moment in the Gospel of John — they became a mirror of our own lives.

We had stumbled, and more than once. We had broken trust, betrayed our own convictions, and wounded each other deeply. And yet... we were not cast out. Like the woman caught in sin and dragged before the temple courts, we, too, felt the stones of condemnation being gathered around us; some thrown by others, many by ourselves. But just as in the Gospel, Jesus bent down, drew something only Heaven could interpret in the dust, and lifted our heads with those life-changing words: *"Neither do I condemn you."*

Mercy for the Moment,
Grace for the Journey

Forgiveness is not a wipe-it-clean-and-forget moment. It is a holy unravelling of guilt, a sacred invitation to become something different, something redeemed. Mercy met us in our lowest places. Grace walked with us as we stood up again. That's the beauty of Jesus' statement — the balance of divine compassion and divine commission. *You are forgiven.* That is mercy. *Go and sin no more.* That is grace — the power to live differently, to be different.

For a long time, I believed forgiveness was only about cancelling a debt. But life has shown me it's also about restoration, about helping the forgiven remember they are worthy of living whole again. In our marriage, we had to accept this divine forgiveness and then practice forgiving each other. Again and again. Some days were full of hope, others felt like starting over. And yet we heard Jesus' voice over our own failure: *"You are forgiven."*

When Stones Fall to the Ground

The scene in John 8 is astonishing. One by one, the accusers walk away. The woman remains, waiting perhaps for Jesus to speak the words of judgment she expects. But instead, He affirms her worth. She was guilty, yes. But she was also seen. Loved. Worth saving.

There is a moment in every marriage where you have to choose: will I be an accuser or an advocate? Will I pick up stones, or will I stay long enough to look into the eyes of my partner and say, "I don't condemn you either"?

It was not easy. It meant laying down pride, assumptions, fears. It meant opening old wounds so they could finally be cleaned and healed. And it meant choosing to walk away from the stones, the ones we were tempted to throw and the ones we feared would be thrown at us.

The Weight We Carried

There were moments we could hardly speak to each other without tension. The silence became heavier than any shout could have been. We both knew our part in the unraveling. We both knew the promises broken and the tenderness lost. And I remember wondering, "How do we go back?" But that was never the question Jesus asked. He didn't ask her to go back to her innocence or her past. He told her to go forward, without the shame, without the sin.

That forward motion was our calling too. We could not erase the past, but we could choose not to live in it. We could decide what story we would write from that point on. Forgiveness became the ink. Grace, the pen.

Learning to Walk Again

Jesus didn't just forgive the woman, He gave her permission to change. That part, *"Go and sin no more,"* was not a threat or a test. It was an invitation to transformation. It was as if He was saying, "You are no longer who they said you were. Now walk like the woman I see, the one you're becoming."

That's what we learned in the years that followed. We had to learn to walk again, as husband and wife, and as people of faith. We had to rebuild trust, piece by piece. Some days it felt like we were limping. Other days, like we were dancing. But always, we were moving forward.

I remember one morning early in our healing journey. We were in the kitchen, and Stephen reached out, touched my hand gently, and simply said, "Thank you." I asked him what for, and he replied, "For staying. For believing God could still do something with us." I couldn't say anything in response. I just held his hand tighter.

A Sacred Invitation

We often think of Jesus' words as final, *"Go and sin no more."* But I've come to see them as ongoing. Every day we're offered that invitation. Every day we're reminded: you're not stuck in your past. You don't have to repeat the same cycles. You are not defined by the lowest moments of your life. You are forgiven. Now go. Live. Love. Choose differently.

This became especially real when we looked at one day being blessed with a family. The responsibility of raising them in grace while having walked through so much brokenness ourselves was daunting. But it also gave us hope. If God could redeem our marriage, He could use it to teach our growing family what mercy looks like in action. What grace feels like when it's costly and powerful. What love looks like when it's chosen, not just felt.

The Freedom of the Uncondemned

When you've been forgiven much, you begin to understand freedom. Not the freedom to do whatever you want, but the freedom to live without the weight of shame. That freedom is sacred. And we never want to take it for granted.

We look at each other now — older, wiser, still growing — and we marvel at what God has done. We shouldn't be here, not really. If statistics had their way, if bitterness had been allowed to bloom, if shame had had the last word, our story would have ended differently. But mercy rewrote the script. Grace gave us a new chapter. And Jesus, just as He did for that woman so long ago, lifted our heads and reminded us: we are not condemned.

Scriptures that Spoke to Our Journey

- **John 8:10-11** – "Jesus straightened up and asked her, 'Woman, where are they? Has no one condemned you?' 'No one, sir,' she said. 'Then neither do I condemn you,' Jesus declared. 'Go now and leave your life of sin.'"
- **Isaiah 1:18** – "Come now, let us reason together, says the Lord. Though your sins are like scarlet, they shall be as white as snow."
- **Romans 8:1** – "There is now no condemnation for those who are in Christ Jesus."
- **2 Corinthians 5:17** – "Therefore, if anyone is in Christ, the new creation has come: The old has gone, the new is here!"
- **Micah 7:18-19** – "Who is a God like you, who pardons sin and forgives the transgression... You will again have compassion on us; you will tread our sins underfoot and hurl all our iniquities into the depths of the sea."

A Story Still Being Written

Stephen and I are not perfect. But we are forgiven. And every day, we choose to walk in that forgiveness. To live out the second chance we've been given. To love each other with the kind of love that Christ showed to a woman caught in sin, to two broken spouses trying to rebuild, and to everyone who's ever needed to hear those words:

You are forgiven. Go and sin no more.

CHAPTER ELEVEN

THE LONG ROAD HOME

Healing is often mistaken for a moment. But for us, healing was a process. A journey. A series of ordinary, holy choices made over and over again.

There were no trumpets announcing that they had crossed some invisible finish line. No magical day where everything was suddenly easy. Instead, healing came gently, in rhythms. In the little things.

It came in laughter—the first real laugh after a season of tears. It startled them. Both of them paused, and then they laughed again. It was like breathing fresh air after being underwater.

It came in shared meals—when Stephen started helping in the kitchen, when they sat across from each other without a wall of silence between them. When they gave thanks, not just for food, but for one more day together.

It came in rediscovery, finding new ways to connect. New books. New worship playlists. New walks in the evening where they talked about their dreams again instead of their wounds. They were learning how to live, not just how to survive.

There were setbacks too. Days when trust trembled. When fear whispered old lies. When they reacted from their old wounds instead of their new hope. But even then, healing showed up, in apologies given quickly, in forgiveness offered without conditions, in the way they reached for each other rather than pulling away.

Counseling helped. So did community. They surrounded themselves with people who didn't expect perfection but reminded them of progress. People who prayed with them and for them. Who celebrated the wins and sat with them in the hard.

Stephen began to serve, not from a place of performance, but from a heart that had been humbled and healed. Krystina began to live again, walls crumbling down and words she never had poured into her spirit.

Intimacy was restored slowly. Tenderly. With trust and patience. They learned each other's rhythms again. They spoke new love languages—ones shaped by healing, not pain. It was not what it had been before—but in many ways, it was better. Deeper. Real.

They began to dream forward. They talked about the future, not with dread, but with hope. They started praying for other couples. Their wounds became wisdom. Their story, once almost silenced by shame, became a song of redemption.

Healing did not erase what had happened. But it redefined it. The pain no longer had the final word. Grace did.

What once felt like the end of their story became the beginning of a new chapter. A chapter not built on perfection, but on promise. Not a fairytale, but a faithful tale.

This is what healing looked like. Not instant. But intentional. Not flawless. But faithful.

A love that kept showing up, again and again.

Even after.

Healing is more than relief from pain. It is restoration. Reclaiming what was lost. Rebuilding what was broken. It is the journey back to wholeness, spirit, soul, and body.

But healing does not just happen to us. It is something we must want.

It's striking that in John 5, Jesus approaches a man who had been ill for thirty-eight years and asks him a question that seems almost absurd: *"Do you want to be healed?"* Surely the answer is obvious. He is lying on a mat beside the pool of Bethesda, waiting for a miracle. Why would Jesus even ask?

Because healing is not passive.

Healing begins with desire, a holy discontent with the brokenness. We can grow comfortable in dysfunction. We can adapt to our pain and make it our identity. Sometimes we carry our wounds so long they feel like part of us. Jesus, in asking the question, invites us to search our hearts: *Do you want to be well? Are you willing to lay aside your excuses, your pride, your fears? Will you partner with Me in the process of becoming whole?*

Stephen and Krystina had to answer that question too. *Do you want to be healed?* It was not just about surviving the fallout of secrets or restoring what had been lost; it was about participating in the renewal God wanted to bring. It meant facing hard truths. Surrendering control. Trusting that the slow work of grace would be enough.

Healing required them to be involved. To show up. To walk out their wholeness one step at a time. There were things Jesus could only do in them, but there were also choices they had to make. To forgive. To stay. To believe again. To get up when they fell. To take hold of the hand stretched out to them.

One of the clearest portraits of Christ's ministry is found in Matthew 15:30:

> *Many people came to Him. They brought with them those who were not able to walk. They brought those who were not able to see. They brought those who were not able to hear or speak and many others. Then they put them at the feet of Jesus and He healed them.*

They came. Broken. Burdened. Desperate. They brought others. They came for healing. And He healed them.

This is not just an ancient report, it is a timeless promise.

There is healing in Jesus. And there is no shame in needing it. You are not alone. The man who could not walk. The woman who could not stop bleeding. The child who was tormented. The blind. The voiceless. The forgotten. *Many* came to Him. And He healed them all.

Krystina and Stephen came to that realization: He would heal them too, if they came to Him.

Healing does not mean forgetting. It means being free. Free to feel joy again. Free to hope. Free to love without fear. Free to live without shame.

Healing does not erase the past. But it transforms it.
Your scars become stories of survival.
Your wounds become wells of wisdom.
Your pain becomes a platform for purpose.

Healing is not always fast. It is rarely linear. But it is real. And it is available.

It is a Person.

And He is asking still, *"Do you want to be healed?"*

CHAPTER TWELVE

PUTTING ON THE WHOLE ARMOR OF GOD

Marriage is not merely a contract or a companionship—it is a covenant. And every covenant, especially one so central to God's design, will be contested. This chapter is about learning to fight—not against one another—but together, against the real enemy. Stephen and Krystina came to understand that the trials they faced were not just emotional or circumstantial, but spiritual. Their wounds were not only of the heart, but also of the spirit, and their healing required more than therapy, love, or even time. It required God. And not just passively inviting Him in, but actively suiting up in His armor.

The Apostle Paul, writing to the Ephesians, said,

> *"Put on the full armor of God, so that you can take your stand against the devil's schemes"* (Ephesians 6:11).

For Stephen and Krystina, this was no longer a poetic metaphor. It was instruction. It was a battle strategy. Their relationship had already weathered storms. But if they were going to build a life of lasting intimacy and spiritual fruitfulness, they needed to be spiritually armed.

Waking Up to the Battle

At first, they had been like many couples, reactive, confused by the cycles of conflict that seemed to return again and again. Sometimes it was a miscommunication, sometimes a sense of emotional distance, sometimes the triggering of past traumas. But as they matured in faith, they began to notice a pattern. The most intense conflicts often came right before or after a spiritual breakthrough. After a beautiful moment of unity. Or before a key decision in their business or family life. Slowly, they began to realize: this was warfare.

Stephen recalled how easily he had once slipped into hopelessness and isolation. Krystina remembered how fragile her heart could feel, how quickly she would spiral into thoughts of inadequacy or fear. But this time, they responded differently. Rather than drawing back, they began drawing near, first to God, then to each other.

The Armor Becomes Real

The armor of God stopped being a Sunday school topic and became a lifestyle. They would rise early and pray. Not always perfectly. Sometimes one of them was sleepy. Sometimes one was angry. But they pressed on. Over time, their prayers grew deeper and more attuned to each other's struggles. They started reading Scripture together and claiming God's promises. When accusations whispered in the night: "You are not enough," "This will never work," "They will never change", they began to recognize the source: the accuser of the brethren.

And so, they clothed themselves.

The Belt of Truth

This became the foundation. In their marriage, it meant complete honesty—not only about facts, but about fears, weaknesses, and temptations. Stephen had once feared being honest would lead to rejection. Krystina had feared being vulnerable would make her look weak. But truth became their belt, holding everything else in place. When temptation came, they confronted it with truth. When insecurities arose, they spoke truth over each other.

The Breastplate of Righteousness

This was not their own righteousness, but Christ's. Stephen struggled for years with guilt and shame over his past. Krystina battled guilt too, especially about moments she had failed to love well or had been impatient. But righteousness was not something they earned. It was a covering they accepted. The breastplate guarded their hearts from condemnation. It allowed them to walk in grace and extend that grace to one another.

Feet Fitted with the Readiness of the Gospel of Peace

Peace, they learned, was not the absence of conflict. It was the presence of Christ. Their feet had to be ready—to walk into hard conversations, to walk away from offense, to walk humbly even when pride screamed. They had to be quick to apologize, quick to forgive, quick to bring peace. They had to be intentional about creating a home where peace was pursued, not passively hoped for.

The Shield of Faith

Faith became their shield. There were moments when hope faltered. Times when circumstances seemed bleak. When bills piled up. When misunderstandings resurfaced. When old wounds ached. But faith said, "God is still with us." Faith blocked the flaming arrows of doubt. It allowed them to trust in the unseen, to remember who their enemy really was, and who their Defender was. They would hold hands and declare, "This marriage is God's idea. He will complete the work He started in us."

The Helmet of Salvation

Thoughts can be a battlefield. The mind races with scenarios, fears, false narratives. Krystina sometimes imagined Stephen withdrawing because he no longer cared. Stephen sometimes assumed Krystina's silence meant disapproval. The helmet of salvation reminded them who they were: saved, redeemed, new creations. It guarded their thoughts, filtered their perceptions, and reminded them that their story was not over. They had been rescued. And their Redeemer was writing a beautiful chapter.

The Sword of the Spirit

Finally, they learned to fight back. Not with hurtful words or passive aggression, but with the Word of God. Scripture became their sword. When fear rose, they declared, "God has not given us a spirit of fear." When lies came, they quoted, "I am fearfully and wonderfully made." They started journaling verses specific to their marriage and praying them aloud. The Word was not abstract—it was a weapon. It gave them vocabulary for victory.

Praying in the Spirit at All Times

Paul concludes the armor passage by urging believers to "pray in the Spirit on all occasions." This became their habit. Not every prayer was long. Sometimes it was a whispered "Help us, Lord" before a tough conversation. Other times, they would stop and pray in the car, in the kitchen, or before bed. These prayers didn't just invite God into the room; they invited Him into the fight.

Stronger Together

One of the most beautiful revelations was this: they were never meant to fight alone. Marriage was designed for unity, not independence. When one was weary, the other held the shield. When one struggled to pray, the other lifted them up. They were partners in purpose, comrades in arms. The enemy may have tried to sow division, but God had planted unity.

This new awareness changed everything. Even in the heat of disagreement, they would sometimes pause and say, "Wait. This is not about us." And suddenly, the enemy's tactics became visible. Division, offense, fear—these were his weapons. But theirs were stronger. Love, truth, peace, righteousness, faith, salvation, and the Word of God.

Preparing for the Future

Spiritual warfare wasn't just for the crises of the past. It was for the future. Parenthood, ministry, finances, family—each would bring new challenges. But now they were prepared. They were not perfect. But they were protected. They were not invincible. But they were armed.

And more than anything, they were united.

The Beauty of Standing Firm

There is a quiet power in standing. Sometimes victory is not in conquering, but in withstanding. In refusing to give up. In holding ground when everything tempts you to walk away. Stephen and Krystina had walked through fire. But now, they stood. Together. In faith. In love. In the armor of God.

Their marriage became more than just a testimony of redemption. It became a fortress. A refuge. A light to others. And not because they were strong, but because they had learned to fight with God, not against each other.

Conclusion

The battle of marriage is real. But so is the victory. And the victory belongs not to the strongest or the smartest, but to those who are willing to suit up daily in the armor of God. To choose truth over illusion. Righteousness over resentment. Peace over chaos. Faith over fear. Salvation over shame. And the Word over lies.

Stephen and Krystina did not emerge from the battlefield unscathed. But they emerged together. And stronger. And now, clothed in the armor of God, they stood ready, not just to survive, but to thrive.

And in that, they found not only healing, but holy ground.

CHAPTER THIRTEEN

RESTORED INTIMACY: BODY, SOUL AND SPIRIT

For Stephen and Krystina, intimacy was once a fragile thread, easily frayed by mistrust, emotional detachment, and years of misunderstanding. But healing had taken root, and from this restored ground, true intimacy could grow again—not the counterfeit kind that simply mimics closeness, but the kind that is born of vulnerability, safety, and God's presence.

Intimacy Begins in the Spirit

Before the body ever responds, the spirit must awaken. Spiritual intimacy is the first and most foundational layer of restored marital closeness. It is the sacred agreement between two souls to walk in the light with God and with each other. When Stephen began to take leadership in prayer, opening their days and closing their nights in communion with the Lord, something shifted in Krystina. She felt safe. Not just physically, but spiritually. He wasn't merely chasing God for his own sake; he was covering her in that same pursuit.

The truth is, no marriage can sustain deep intimacy without spiritual unity. When a couple prays together, studies God's Word together, and surrenders their individual wills to divine purpose, walls come down that even therapy cannot dismantle. The wounds Stephen had inflicted through betrayal and secrecy were not simply healed through conversation—they were sanctified through worship. Each time they invited God into their private world, it became less private and more sacred.

Spiritual intimacy also meant accountability. They no longer let offenses linger or justified cold silences. They were learning to forgive quickly, to confess early, and to pursue reconciliation with urgency. The Word became their compass. When their thoughts or emotions ran wild, they had an anchor. They were growing in the understanding that spiritual union was not about perfection but pursuit—pursuit of God and pursuit of one another.

Soul Ties Rewritten

Beyond the spirit is the soul—the seat of emotions, thoughts, and personality. If the spirit is the lamp that guides, the soul is the canvas on which love is painted. But for years, Stephen and Krystina's soul ties had been frayed. Disappointments, harsh words, unmet needs, and unspoken fears had dulled the colors of their relationship. Restoring this soul connection required both honesty and patience.

They began to speak differently to one another. Stephen listened with intention instead of defense. Krystina learned to share her needs without guilt. Their emotional intimacy blossomed not in grand moments but in quiet ones—over shared meals, long walks, or conversations early in the morning on the back porch. They revisited their dreams, their fears, their joys. The emotional distance that had once felt permanent began to close inch by inch, word by word.

Healing of the soul also meant breaking unhealthy patterns. Where fear had dictated silence, now there was courage. Where guilt had muzzled expression, now there was grace. They started writing new emotional scripts for their marriage. The narrative was no longer shame and survival; it was vulnerability and connection.

In the soul space, laughter returned. Inside jokes came back. There were random texts during the day just to say, "I'm thinking of you." They remembered why they liked each other. Not just loved—but liked. In many marriages, the soul is forgotten because it is not as measurable as physical touch or as holy as spiritual disciplines. But it is just as crucial. The soul is where we feel seen, understood, and chosen.

The Body Responds to Safety

Only when the spirit and soul find their rhythm can the body fully respond in intimacy. For Stephen and Krystina, this meant that physical closeness was no longer about performance or obligation—it was about celebration. Their bodies now spoke a language that aligned with their hearts and spirits. The awkwardness that sometimes follows long seasons of detachment began to fade, and in its place came a rediscovery of joy, delight, and passion.

The physical act of intimacy became a liturgy of unity, a physical echo of all that had been restored. No longer burdened by shame or resentment, they could meet each other with openness. They did not rush this. They were intentional, gentle, and kind. The process of restoring physical intimacy mirrored the story of their entire healing—grace upon grace.

Sex within marriage is not only sacred but prophetic. It speaks of oneness, covenant, and pleasure ordained by God. The Song of Solomon paints a vibrant picture of this kind of union—full of desire, affirmation, and delight. It is not accidental that Scripture begins with the joining of man and woman in the Garden and ends with the marriage supper of the Lamb. Intimacy is part of the divine narrative, and when redeemed, it becomes one of the most powerful testimonies of God's restorative power.

Breaking False Narratives

Krystina had once believed that intimacy was dangerous—that vulnerability would only lead to pain. Stephen had associated intimacy with performance, something to prove or use as a way to mask brokenness. These were lies they had picked up through past wounds, culture, and personal failure. But now, truth was rewriting their story.

They realized that restored intimacy is not about perfection but connection. It is not about getting it all right every time but being willing to try again, to listen again, to love again. They gave each other permission to be human—to not always know, to sometimes be awkward, to not get it right every time.

This grace-filled atmosphere allowed them to explore not only their physical desires but also their longings for comfort, closeness, and affirmation. Touch, once feared or withheld, became a gift again. A held hand. A kiss on the forehead. A warm embrace after a hard day. Each act was a lit candle in the dark spaces of their past.

Biblical Echoes of Intimacy

Throughout the Bible, intimacy is both literal and symbolic. Adam and Eve knew each other and were unashamed. Isaac and Rebekah's love was tender and exclusive. Hosea pursued Gomer not just as an act of obedience but as a symbol of God's relentless love. Even Christ refers to the Church as His Bride, calling us into a deep and eternal communion with Him.

Marriage, in all its intimacy, is a reflection of divine union. Paul's letter to the Ephesians emphasizes this in chapter 5, urging husbands to love their wives as Christ loved the Church—sacrificially, intentionally, and with reverence. Wives are to respond with respect and honor, not as subordinates but as co-heirs in grace. This sacred rhythm of mutuality and love is what Stephen and Krystina were now experiencing.

From Fear to Freedom

Perhaps one of the most miraculous aspects of their story was the movement from fear to freedom. Where there had once been suspicion, there was now security. Where there had been avoidance, there was now pursuit. They were not just having better conversations or better intimacy —they were learning to *abide* in each other's presence with joy and expectation.

They also learned that restored intimacy does not mean that every day is perfect. There are still off days, tired moments, and miscommunications. But now, they fight together, not against each other. They understand that intimacy must be nurtured, protected, and valued.

A Sacred Garden Reopened

In many ways, intimacy is like a garden. It can grow wild with weeds if left unattended. It can become dry in seasons of drought. But when tended with care, it becomes a place of beauty, life, and flourishing. Stephen and Krystina were once locked out of that garden, standing outside its gates with regret and longing. But God, in His mercy, reopened the gate.

Restored intimacy became their new Eden. A place of laughter and rest, vulnerability and joy, shared silence and passionate reconnection. It was not just about feeling good—it was about becoming whole. They were not merely husband and wife. They were partners in covenant, lovers in rhythm, and co-heirs of grace.

PART IV

THE STANDING

CHAPTER FOURTEEN

HONORING OUR ROOTS

You don't arrive at the altar alone. You come carrying names, voices, habits, wounds, and blessings. You bring your family with you—not physically, but in your soul. In your tone of voice. In your expectations. In the way you fold towels or the way you handle conflict. We didn't always see it at first, but now we know: our marriage began long before we ever met. It began in the homes we were raised in.

Our parents—each in their own way—loved us. Imperfectly, yes. But genuinely. They provided, they protected, they prayed. They didn't always get it right. Some lessons were taught by wisdom. Others, by silence. Some of our pain has echoes that go back to them. And yet, so does much of our strength.

We grew up thinking that marriage looked a certain way, often because of what we saw—or didn't see—at home. One of us learned that conflict was dangerous and must be avoided at all costs. The other learned that shouting meant love was still alive. One of us saw affection withheld when expectations weren't met. We didn't realize it then, but our parents were laying foundations in us. Some strong. Some cracked. All human.

And yet, they were ordained by God to raise us.

We see now that parenting has always been complex, even in Scripture. Isaac favored Esau, Rebekah conspired with Jacob. David was a man after God's heart, but he failed many of his sons. Eli was a priest, but his sons defiled the altar. Even Mary and Joseph—though chosen for the highest calling, lost track of young Jesus on the way home from the temple.

Perfection was never the standard. Obedience was. And love. And repentance.

In many ways, our parents did the best they could with what they had. They gave us life, education, provided for us, and prayers that we are only now beginning to appreciate. Yes, there were deficits. We inherited some unspoken burdens. But we also developed resilience, grit, faith, and a commitment to family that has shaped our own.

Now that we are desiring to be parents ourselves, we understand more than ever the quiet sacrifices they made. The sleepless nights. The fears they never voiced. The apologies they didn't know how to offer. The love they gave, even when we couldn't recognize it as such.

We've had to sort through what to carry forward and what to lay down. We've chosen to honor the legacy and also to redeem it so that in the future, by the grace of God, our future family will inherit more wholeness than we did. This is the work of every generation: to bless what was good, and to heal what was not.

And so, to our parents, we say this:

Thank you.
Thank you for giving us the best of yourselves.
Thank you for your faith, your tears, your resilience.
We forgive the places where you fell short.
And we bless you for the ways you stood tall.

Because of you, we have learned what it means to endure.
Because of you, we now know what it means to choose love, again and again.
You were not perfect. But you were purposed.

And now, we stand—your children—ready to carry the baton forward with humility and grace.

CHAPTER FIFTEEN

CALLED TO MOTHERHOOD

There are many things people prepare for—weddings, careers, exams. But how do you prepare to carry eternity in your arms?

Krystina

As I grew up, the thought of *I can't wait to be a mother* never even crossed my mind. Throughout my upbringing, I chose not to involve myself with babies or toddlers. I was drawn to someday being married, but there was no interest to experience pregnancy, have children of my own, or raise a family.

Ever since Stephen and I met, he shared that he was very excited to one day start a family and have kids. He always joked that he wanted twin girls, to which I groaned at the very thought. But he was always extremely patient with me, never trying to guilt, shame, embarrass, or harass me to start a family with him.

For nearly a decade of marriage, I wasn't sure I was ready to say yes. And now because of all that Stephen and I had journeyed through—the shame, the betrayal, the healing, would it be fair to bring a child into something still being rebuilt? Could a home that had once cracked hold new life safely? I feared repeating patterns I had barely just begun to unlearn.

Motherhood is unlike anything else. It's more than biology. More than a milestone. It is a sacred entrustment from God. A calling wrapped in vulnerability. A daily surrender. A holy yes.

And yet, something inside me kept reaching. A small, stubborn hope. A yearning that refused to die. I began to pray—not for a child, but that if God wanted me to be a mother that He was going to have to change my heart. I asked God to prepare me from the inside out. To do something in me first.

Then came a moment that changed everything.

My sister had just had her first child. She lived in California, and I flew out to spend time with her. I told myself I was just going to help, but looking back, I realize I was also searching, perhaps for clarity, for reassurance, for something I couldn't name. And then I held her. My niece. This impossibly tiny, perfect human, breathing softly against my chest; smiling at me like she already loved me.

Something melted in me.

There was no fear in her eyes. Just trust. Just being. I didn't need to have answers in that moment. I just needed to *be there*. And in that stillness, I felt God whisper: *"This is what you were made for; not control, not perfection. Just presence. Stewardship. Love."*

I began to see motherhood not as a destination, but as an offering.

Back home, I scouted the Scriptures like a woman digging for water in a dry land. I needed to know: what did God ask of mothers? What did it look like to mother *with* Him?

One name came to mind—Mary. A young woman, likely a teenager, not married, certainly not prepared by human standards. Yet she heard the most incredible words ever spoken to a woman: *"You will bear a son... He will be great and will be called the Son of the Most High... the government will be on His shoulders."*

How does a girl carry that?

She didn't panic. She didn't protest. She simply said, *"Let it be to me according to Your word."*

Mary didn't mother from a place of knowing; she mothered from a place of *trust*. She wasn't asked to understand the whole plan, only to carry what was given to her, with grace.

Then there was Jochebed, the mother of Moses. She, too, knew her child was special, just not *how* special. She dared to believe when everything around her screamed despair. She risked everything to preserve the life of her son, not because she had seen the Red Sea part, but because she had seen something in her baby boy. A spark. A promise. And she protected that promise at all costs.

And Ruth, faithful, kind, unlikely. She wasn't even an Israelite, yet she chose covenant. She followed Naomi into a future she couldn't see. She married again, bore a son named Obed. Obed fathered Jesse. Jesse fathered David. And David's line led to Christ.

Ruth's womb became the hidden passage of redemption.

All these women, ordinary yet chosen. Mothers who said yes to something far bigger than themselves. That's when I understood: *this is not about me.* It's never been about me. Children don't belong to us. They pass through us. We are not owners—we are *guardians of destiny.*

We don't get to decide what they become, only whether we'll pour ourselves out faithfully while we have them in our arms.

Motherhood is not about achieving something. It is about stewarding *someone.*

That realization brought freedom. I felt less pressure to be a perfect mother. I felt the call to be a present one. To show up with love. To be a resting place for little souls who don't yet know how to name the world around them.

I knew then that my job wasn't to save them from every storm—but to be a lighthouse when the waters rise.

Stephen and I began to pray intentionally—not just for children, but for *who we would become* as their parents. We fasted, we repented, we read Scriptures aloud. We asked God to clean our bloodline, to bless our womb and our lineage. To start a new cycle through us.

Motherhood, I learned, doesn't begin when a child is born. It begins when your heart opens wide enough to say: *"Let it be unto me, according to Your word."*

And so, we wait—sometimes with tears, sometimes with laughter—but always with hope.

For motherhood is not a reward for getting life right. It is a calling entrusted to those willing to walk humbly with God.

CHAPTER SIXTEEN

MERCY AND GRACE: THE TWO SIDES OF REDEMPTION

Stephen

There came a point in our journey when the difference between mercy and grace became more than theological. It became deeply personal. We did not learn it in a Bible study or from a well-crafted sermon. We discovered it in the quiet, raw moments when we were most vulnerable. In our silence. In our failures. In the prayers we whispered through tears. In the moments when kindness found us unexpectedly and asked for nothing in return. That is where we began to see it. Mercy and grace were not interchangeable. They were not synonyms. They were companions. They were the arms of God that held us in different ways at different times.

At the beginning, we often used those words as if they meant the same thing. Mercy. Grace. Forgiveness. Love. It all felt like one flood of God's goodness covering what we feared would destroy us. But as we walked further down this road of healing, we saw it more clearly. Mercy withheld what we deserved. Grace gave us what we could never earn.

Mercy Held Us Together

Krystina

Mercy came first. Mercy met me on the cold tile of the bathroom floor, when pain wrapped around me like a second skin. It did not ignore the sin. It did not pretend the damage did not exist. But it did something I did not expect.

I remember one night crying out in the dark, not even sure it was a prayer. It felt more like a gasp. I did not ask for anything specific. I just needed to be seen. I needed to know if I was still allowed to hope. What came was not thunder. And it was not silence either. It was a strange and holy stillness. My spirit heard the words "trust me." In that moment I knew I was held. Not excused. Not overlooked. But held.

In Him mercy met me, and He placed this verse in my heart: "The LORD is close to the broken-hearted; he rescues those whose spirits are crushed" (Psalm 34:18).

Stephen felt it too. He says that one of the clearest moments of mercy came during a conversation we had when things were still incredibly fragile. He had no words to make it right. No reasons that could undo the pain. He expected me to be furious. Honestly, I was. But I also saw his eyes. He was breaking too. I found myself saying, "I do not know how we will move forward, but I do not want to punish you. I want to understand." That was not rehearsed. It came from somewhere deeper than logic. That was mercy.

Mercy stands in the space between the offense and the consequence. It does not pretend the betrayal was insignificant. It simply chooses not to retaliate. It gives room for repentance to breathe.

In Scripture, I think of the woman caught in adultery. The crowd was right, technically. She had broken the law. Stones were ready. But Jesus bent down and He looked at her, not with accusation, but with compassion. "Has no one condemned you? Then neither do I. Go and sin no more." That was mercy. Not a denial of her sin. A delay of destruction. A breath of hope.

Grace Rebuilt What Was Broken

Stephen

I want to clarify a couple words that get used interchangeably, but have very different meaning and application. Mercy is not receiving the punishment we deserve for a decision and or behaviour. It is a free gift of the perspective that our identity is not based on our past faults and mistakes. We make mistakes, but we are not a mistake. We make bad decisions, but we aren't a bad person because of that.

But grace is radically different. And when grace showed up, it felt different.

Grace is wild. Grace is undeserved favour. Grace is a supernatural equipping from the Holy Spirit to think and behave beyond our own capacity, ability, and understanding. Grace is not content to just let us go free. Grace wants to walk us home and throw a party when we arrive.

Krystina found grace on an ordinary afternoon. She was doing dishes and I walked by and said something that made her laugh. Not a polite laugh. A real one. I had not heard that sound from her in a long time. In that moment, I felt grace. Not because everything was fixed. But because joy had shown up without needing permission.

I saw grace when I realized God was not just tolerating me. I thought mercy meant God would love me just enough to get by. But grace was different. Grace said, I still have work for you. I still trust you with your destiny. Because of your past and allowing grace to enter into you, I can now use you. Grace gave me a vision of my identity through the eyes of my Heavenly Father.

Grace clothed the prodigal son in a robe and gave him a ring. Grace did not ask him to serve as a slave. It restored him as a son. Grace turned Peter's denial into his calling. Grace walked Ruth into Boaz's field. Grace found David after Bathsheba and still called him a man after God's heart.

Mercy says, You can go free. Grace says, Come sit at my table.

For both of us, grace was found in the moments when we dared to believe in new beginnings. Not pretending the past never happened. But believing that it no longer defined our future. Grace gave us permission to dream again. To try again. To risk again.

The Tension Between the Two

Stephen

I struggled with both. Mercy made me feel unworthy. Grace made me uncomfortable. I had grown up with the idea that failure meant disqualification. I could not understand a God who spoke gently after disobedience. I kept waiting for the correction. It never came. Instead, grace kept handing him tools to rebuild. And mercy kept holding off the punishment I thought would surely come.

Krystina

I had my own fears. I thought accepting grace too quickly meant I was minimizing the pain. I did not want to move on too fast and miss the depth of what had happened. But what I learned is that grace does not erase pain. It transforms it. Grace does not ask us to pretend. It asks us to trust.

Why Both Matter

Mercy without grace can leave us forgiven, but hollow. Like a criminal who has been acquitted, but has no home to return to. Grace without mercy can feel shallow. Like a beautiful house built on broken ground. We needed both.

We felt this most deeply one evening at a prayer meeting. David and Hope, who had walked with us through our hardest seasons, asked if we wanted to bless one another. At first, I hesitated. I was afraid I would cry. Stephen already was. I took his hands and began to speak. I said, "I bless you to be the man God called you to be. I bless your courage. I bless your heart. I bless your future."

Stephen says he could barely breathe. Those words cracked something open. Not because he felt worthy. But because he knew he was not. And that is what grace does. It gives what we cannot earn.

Stephen looked at me with tears and said, "Thank you for not giving up on me. I bless your heart to heal fully. I bless your joy. I bless the years ahead of us. May they be marked by grace." That moment was holy. Mercy kissed grace. And our story began again.

Biblical Echoes

Stephen

We see both mercy and grace throughout Scripture. In Exodus, God describes Himself as compassionate and gracious, slow to anger and abounding in steadfast love. The Hebrew word for mercy carries the image of deep, womb-like compassion. The word for grace speaks of favor and generosity.

Jesus embodied both. He extended mercy to the accused and grace to the hungry. He forgave the thief and promised him paradise. He touched the leper and restored him to community.

Paul wrote that it is by grace we are saved, through faith, not by works. But he also described God as rich in mercy. We need both. We are saved because mercy withheld judgment and grace poured out life.

Living the Difference

Krystina

Today, we live in the light of both mercy and grace. When we counsel others in their valleys, we do not rush to fix. We listen. We sit with them. We remind them that God's mercies are new every morning.

Then, slowly, we speak grace. We talk about what still can be. We tell them joy can return. That dreams can be resurrected. That favor is not just for the perfect.

I often say, Mercy found me on the bathroom floor. Grace helped me stand again.

Stephen adds, mercy said I was not condemned. Grace said I was going to be empowered to complete my God ordained destiny.

Our story is not about what went wrong anymore. It is about the love that put it right again. A love that knew when to withhold and when to give. A love full of mercy. A love overflowing with grace.

CHAPTER SEVENTEEN

HAPPILY EVEN AFTER

When people talk about marriage, they often end with the phrase "happily ever after." It sounds tidy, fairy-tale perfect. But what they don't tell you is that "ever after" can have valleys as deep as its mountains are high. What they don't say is that sometimes you break before you bend. That sometimes "ever after" includes tears you never thought you'd cry, and silence louder than words.

But by the grace of God, Stephen and I have come to know a deeper joy. Not the kind born from perfection, but the kind born from redemption. This is our *happily even after*.

There was a time we couldn't imagine saying that. There were moments we thought we wouldn't make it. Days we doubted whether love was strong enough to rebuild what had been broken. Nights we wrestled with God, begging Him for clarity and strength. But this story—our story—is not about how perfectly we walked through pain. It is about how perfectly God showed up in our weakness.

A God Who Sees

Krystina

There was a day, I remember vividly, when I was sitting in the car and I couldn't bring myself to go inside; heart pounding, tears running down my face. I was too broken to pretend everything was fine. I had questions without answers. But in that still moment, I felt something I hadn't felt in a long time—seen. Not judged. Not corrected. Seen.

It reminded me of Hagar in the wilderness. She wasn't Sarah. She wasn't the promise bearer. She was the outsider who ran away in pain and confusion. But God met her there, and she called Him the God who sees.

The first whisper that even in the wilderness of our marriage, we were not alone. Our Father Who saw us, said "Trust me."

The Grace That Covers

Stephen

I had my own journey. There were things I had to face—regrets, pride, shame. I didn't need a judge. I needed a Savior. And slowly, grace became more than a word we used in church. It became the lifeline that pulled us both out of the water.

Grace didn't pretend the wounds weren't real. It simply refused to let them define our ending. It reminded us that God doesn't discard the broken. He redeems them. That He doesn't just repair what's fractured. Sometimes, He creates something entirely new from the ashes.

I think of Peter, the disciple who swore he'd never deny Jesus and then did—three times. When he realized what he'd done, he wept bitterly. But Jesus didn't shame him. He invited him to breakfast. He didn't erase Peter's past. He redeemed it by calling him to feed His sheep. I held onto that story like an anchor. Because if Jesus could restore Peter, He could restore us too.

The Mercy That Holds

Krystina

Grace gave us what we didn't deserve. But it was mercy that withheld what we did deserve. And that distinction changed everything.

There were times I wanted to keep a record of wrongs. Times I felt justified in my pain. But mercy whispered, "Let go." Mercy taught me that healing wasn't about fairness. It was about freedom.

Stephen

It reminded me of the woman caught in adultery. They wanted to stone her. They had every legal right. But Jesus stooped down, wrote in the dirt, and turned the situation upside down. He didn't condone her sin. He covered her shame. He didn't say, "You're fine." He said, "Go and sin no more." That blend of mercy and truth became the template for how Krystina and I chose to walk forward—imperfectly, but with eyes fixed on Jesus.

Small Steps, Big Miracles

The road back to one another was not marked by grand gestures. It was paved by small acts of faith. Apologies spoken with trembling voices. Honest conversations that stripped us bare. Prayers whispered together at night when neither of us knew what to say. Every step mattered.

There was the first time we laughed again without forcing it. The first time we reached for each other's hand and felt peace instead of pressure. The first time we shared our story with someone else, not from a place of shame, but from hope.

We watched as God used our scars to encourage others. We saw how the place of our deepest failure became the wellspring of compassion for others walking the same road. Our pain had purpose.

The Ministry of Presence

Along the way, God placed people in our lives who didn't try to fix us. They didn't offer quick answers. They offered presence. They sat with us. Prayed with us. Believed for us when we couldn't believe for ourselves.

We remember one mentor couple, older and full of wisdom, who told us something simple but profound. "The goal is not to be right. The goal is to have unity and peace." That truth blew our minds. We had been fighting to win, not to understand. They painted the picture of a new desire, to truly understand each other and have compassion for one another.

God in the Midst

Scripture is full of people who met God not after the storm—but in the midst of a storm.

Jesus in the boat during the tempest didn't stop the storm before He showed up. He was already there. Shadrach, Meshach, and Abed-nego met Him in the fire. Not after. Not outside. In the middle. And that was our story too.

We didn't wait until everything was neat and tidy to experience God. He met us in our questioning. In our silence. And in our slowly mending hearts. And it was in those moments that we truly began to rebuild—not just our marriage, but our faith, our vision, our hope.

Beauty from Ashes

Krystina

Isaiah 61 talks about the oil of joy for mourning, the garment of praise for a spirit of despair, and beauty for ashes. I used to think that meant the ashes would disappear. But now I see it differently. The ashes are still part of the story. They are the evidence of what burned. But somehow, through the miracle of grace, they become the soil from which something beautiful grows.

Stephen and I are not the same people we were. And I thank God for that. We've been softened. Refined. Humbled. Strengthened. We've learned that love is not a feeling. It's a decision. A covenant. A sacred dance of mercy and truth, grace and growth.

A New Chapter

We don't pretend we have all the answers. But we know the One who does. And we've come to believe that no story is too broken for God to redeem. No relationship too fractured for Him to restore.

Today, when I look at Stephen, I don't just see a husband. I see a warrior. A man who chose to change. Who chose to fight for us. Who chose repentance over pride. And he says the same about me.

And when I look at Krystina, I see someone who had been blessed with a human heart to love me despite it all, but more so a working of the Holy Spirit to both heal and empower her with the grace to trust Him, despite having no reason to trust me.

Now our marriage is not perfect. But it is deeply rooted in something eternal. In Someone Who does not walk away when things fall apart. And in that, we are victorious.

Happily Even After

If you're reading this and wondering if it's too late, if you've gone too far, if the damage is too deep—I want you to know something. There is hope. Not the fluffy kind, but the kind forged in fire. The kind that holds on when everything says to let go.

Stephen and I are living proof that God still writes redemption stories. That grace still wins. That mercy still heals. And that love—real love—can rise again.

So no, our story didn't end with "happily ever after." It's better than that. It's *happily even after*—not because we never failed, but because God never did.

CHAPTER EIGHTEEN

STANDING TOGETHER, STANDING TALL

Stephen

I used to think strength meant never falling. I measured success by how well I could hold everything together, how few cracks I showed. But it turns out, real strength came in the breaking. In the vulnerability. In allowing God to rebuild me from the inside out.

Krystina and I didn't just survive the storm. We didn't merely patch things up. We were rebuilt, reshaped, and realigned by grace. Our foundation now is not just love or compatibility. It is God Himself.

We have learned to stand together in ways we never imagined before. Not because everything is perfect, but because we have discovered the One Who is perfect. The One Who upholds us when we are weak and brings peace when things are turbulent. The One Who whispers, "Stand firm," even when the winds howl around us.

Krystina

For so long, I was terrified of falling apart. I lived with this internal script that told me I had to keep everything steady or it would all unravel. And then it did unravel. But what I thought would be the end became the beginning of something holy.

Our story could have ended in quiet resignation, in two people choosing safety over honesty, or comfort over transformation. But God had other plans. When we said yes to healing, we unknowingly said yes to a new calling. We became more than husband and wife. We became partners in grace, warriors in prayer, and safe havens for each other.

Stephen

We now pray together not out of obligation but out of awe. We have seen what happens when we lean on our own understanding, and we have seen what happens when we surrender. Our prayers used to be individual, sometimes fragmented. Now they are united. We seek God's wisdom not just for our marriage but for our mission.

And yes, we believe we have a mission. Not the flashy kind, but the sacred kind. To live truthfully. To extend grace to others. To mentor those who are walking the road we once limped down. We don't wear our scars as shame but as symbols of God's mercy.

Krystina

There was a moment—not long ago—when we stood at the altar again. Not in front of a crowd, but just the two of us in the quiet of our living room. We spoke new vows. Not to replace the old ones, but to acknowledge where we had been and what we had become. I looked into Stephen's eyes and I saw not the man who had hurt me, but the man who had been remade. And he saw not the woman who had pulled away, but the woman who had returned with a deeper yes.

Stephen

I often think about legacy now. Not just financial or material, but spiritual. Emotional. Relational. What patterns are we breaking? What inheritance are we leaving our future generation? We are determined that the cycles of silence, avoidance, and isolation will end with us.

We are not going to be perfect people. We don't pretend to think we will be. But we are present. We are intentional. We talk about love, about struggle, about God's mercy and our humanity. One day our children will grow up knowing that mistakes do not disqualify them, and that broken things can be made beautiful.

Krystina

One of the most profound shifts has been learning to stand *tall* in forgiveness. Not just once, but daily. I used to think forgiveness was a finish line, something you reached after enough time had passed. But I now know it's a posture. A way of walking. A daily decision to release, to trust, to hope again.

We are not afraid to tell our story anymore. We don't tell it to glorify the pain or spotlight ourselves. We tell it because we believe someone else might be sitting in that same silence we once sat in, wondering if hope still lives here. It does.

Stephen

We are not the same people we were when we first met. Not even close. And that's a good thing. We have been pruned and purified. We have been humbled and healed. We have faced our fears and surrendered our pride. And in that surrender, we have found strength.

Standing together now means listening more, defending less. It means making room for each other's voices, even when they challenge us. It means serving one another without keeping score. It means returning to the Cross again and again, because that's where everything began and everything is sustained.

Krystina

Standing tall does not mean we have no scars. It means we have chosen to rise anyway. It means we have trusted God to use those very scars as instruments of healing for others. It means we are no longer defined by what broke us but by the One who put us back together.

There are still hard days. Of course there are. But they don't shake us like they used to. Because we know where to go. We know how to kneel before we stand. We know that the only way to truly stand tall is to be rooted deep.

Stephen

We dream again. Not just of what we can build but of who we are becoming. And we dream with God, not ahead of Him. We ask Him to lead our steps, to guard our hearts, and to keep us soft toward each other.

And now, when I see Krystina laugh freely, when I see her acceptance of future motherhood, when I hear her voice in prayer, I feel a quiet victory rise in me. Because I know how close we came to losing this. And I know who saved us.

Krystina

There is a peace now. A deep peace. Not because we figured it all out, but because we stopped pretending we could. We stood together through the storm, and now we stand tall because of the One who carried us through it.

Together

Our marriage is not perfect. It is not flawless. But it is real, it is redeemed, and it is deeply rooted in Christ. We are witnesses of what love can do when it is fueled by grace and anchored in truth.

This is our happily even after. Not a fairy tale, but a faith story. Not a finish line, but a fresh beginning every single day.

We stand together. We stand tall. And we give all the glory to God.

THE QUIET MIRACLE

Krystina

Time has a strange tenderness to it. It neither forgets nor rushes healing. And sometimes, without asking permission, it transforms the things we once feared would destroy us into things we now hold with reverence. That's what this journey has become, a sacred story that grew out of the wreckage, a testament to mercy, not merit.

There was a time when I thought we wouldn't make it. When everything inside me ached from disappointment. When I wasn't sure I had the strength to forgive. But something, no, *Someone*, kept whispering: *Just trust Me. You are not alone. Keep walking.* I didn't know then that the walking would become a kind of worship. A way of saying, *I still believe.*

Stephen

I used to think strength looked like confidence, certainty, holding it all together. But I've learned that strength is often found in the trembling voice that says, "I was wrong." In the hand that reaches out when it's not sure it will be taken. In the husband who says, "Let's start again," and the wife who says, "Okay."

I didn't deserve her forgiveness. I still don't. But that's the thing about grace: it's never earned. It's given. Freely. Fiercely. And receiving it will humble you in ways nothing else can. It stripped me of my pride. Then clothed me in purpose.

Krystina

People sometimes ask, "How did you survive it?" And I tell them, "Barefoot. Broken. And by the mercy of God. There were no easy days, no magical turning points. Just ordinary Tuesdays where we chose not to quit. Wednesday mornings with coffee and silence. Thursday evenings filled with awkward prayers and sometimes sacred tears. And slowly, those moments began to stitch our hearts back together.

"We learned to walk again—not as two fractured souls pretending everything was fine—but as partners carrying the same hope. At first, our love limped. But over time, it started to dance again."

Stephen

We still argue. We still misunderstand each other sometimes. But now, we argue with better gentleness. We listen, longer. We fight for us, not against each other. We've learned the holy rhythm of an apology. And laughter—laughter has returned. It's not the naive laughter of a couple untouched by life, but the deep, seasoned kind that knows exactly what it costs to smile again.

Our home has become quieter in some ways. Calmer. There's still music, and stories, and dreams sketched out on napkins. But mostly there is peace. Not perfect peace—but hard-won peace. Peace that was contended for on the battlefield of vulnerability.

Krystina

And no, there are no little feet running down our hallway—yet. There are prayers whispered beneath our breath. Hopes gently held. We are learning not to define fruitfulness by what the world applauds, but by the soil we tend daily—our love, our faith, our service to others.

We don't measure our healing by milestones like pregnancy announcements or anniversaries, but by the softness in our tone when we disagree. By the way we sit close without saying much. By the hand that instinctively reaches for the other in prayer. Those are our miracles.

Stephen

We often talk about destiny now—not just in terms of family or careers, but in the kind of marriage God led us through for the benefit of others. The kind of witness our union bears. We want to be the kind of couple whose story becomes a lighthouse, not a monument. Something that shines for others still lost in a fog, not something polished and untouchable.

If our scars can light someone else's path—then let them shine.

Krystina

We've met couples sitting on the edge of goodbye. Women with hollow eyes asking, "Can love rise again?" Men ashamed to even speak the truth aloud. And when we share our story, we do not romanticize it. We do not wrap it up with a bow. We tell it exactly as it was—ugly, painful, raw—and then we speak of the God who held us both, who never left, who whispered redemption into places we thought were forever ruined.

We tell them, "There is hope. But hope has a name. And His name is Jesus."

Stephen

This story—*our* story—is not a manual. It's not a guarantee. But it is a witness. A signpost. A flicker of light for anyone standing in the aftermath of betrayal, or disappointment, or deep disillusionment. We want you to know: it's not too late. If God could resurrect *this*, He can resurrect *anything*.

But you'll need to lay down your pride. You'll need to pick up your Bible. You'll need to bleed sometimes. And heal sometimes. And you'll need people—counselors, friends, mentors—who will hold you to the light when all you want is to disappear into the dark.

Krystina

I no longer define love as butterflies or passion or compatibility. I define love as *covenant*. As the daily decision to see someone fully and stay. To forgive what your heart doesn't understand. To water the desert places when there is no rain in sight. Love, real love, is quiet. Unshakeable. It is a vow you whisper when no one else is listening.

And now? Now we carry that love like fire in our bones.

Stephen

And so this is our prayer:

If you find yourself here, reading these words and wondering if your marriage has a chance... we pray that our story becomes more than a testimony—it becomes a turning point for yours. That it leads you back to your knees. Back to each other. Back to the God who rewrites stories in the dust of fallen dreams.

We pray that you fight for each other—not perfectly, but faithfully. That you walk barefoot through the wilderness if you must, but always toward home.

We pray that one day, you'll sit together as we do now—not with bitterness, but with quiet gratitude. With bruised hearts still beating strong. With hands that know what it means to hold each other through the storm.

Krystina

We don't know what comes next. Life has its seasons. But this we do know: we were lost, and now we are found. We were wounded, and now we are healing. We were two, and now—we are one.

It is not a fairy tale ending. It is a sacred beginning, again and again.

And we wouldn't trade this quiet miracle for anything.

P.S. We'd love to hear about your journey! Don't hesitate to drop us a line and share your thoughts with us at info@graceevenafter.com

BENEDICTION PRAYER

Lord of restoration,
Thank You for being the Author of our story.
Thank You for every broken piece You have held in Your hands,
for every silence You have filled with grace,
for every wound You have turned into a well of compassion.

May the love we now walk in be a testimony of Your mercy.
Let our marriage be a lighthouse for others lost in the fog of pain,
a whisper to weary hearts that healing is possible,
that forgiveness is not weakness,
that hope is never too far gone.

Teach us, daily, to love like You
with open hands, listening hearts, and anchored faith.
Go before us into the chapters we cannot yet see.
May Your joy be our strength,
and Your peace our song.

In Jesus' name,
Amen.

ABOUT US

Stephen

Stephen was born in Richmond, VA, the child of a young woman and her boyfriend. Brought into this world unexpectedly with parents unprepared, his future had a Providential destiny. Given up for adoption as an infant, his mother desired a traditional and stable home for her firstborn to be raised. Stephen then grew up as a military kid as his father served as a U.S. Air Force fighter pilot and his mother was a teacher before becoming a military spouse, stay-at-home mom and home schooler.

Stephen travelled around the globe as a kid, living and visiting countries like Spain, Turkey, Germany, Italy, and Chile. His adoptive parents were blessed with another child, a daughter quite a few years younger than Stephen. His parents chose to home-school them both throughout their K-12 years, which was a decision based on a life of constantly moving and wanting to instill their values into their kids.

Upon graduation from high-school, Stephen went directly into the workforce full-time, starting in the Defense sector through a unique door being opened by a family friend. He spent over a decade working around the globe in support of the U.S. Military and federal government, with the highlight being deployed as a civilian to Afghanistan.

At age 27, Stephen and Krystina had a whirlwind marriage in Krystina's hometown in southern California. Having been married on a Friday, Stephen began a unique role in Washington D.C. the following Monday. In less than 48 hrs after his wedding, he and Krystina moved to northern Virginia. A few years later, Stephen unexpectedly transitioned from the Defense sector into a technology consultant. Stephen loves his Krystina immensely, is full of expectation in the blessing of fatherhood, and enjoys spending time traveling, trying new foods, and exploring quaint mountain towns around the country.

Krystina

Krystina was born on Edwards Air Force Base in Southern California, the daughter of a U.S. Air Force test pilot and a father who was a senior engineer within the Defense sector. Her mother gained recognition as one of the first female fighter pilots in the U.S. Air Force, and her father rose to the ranks of leading the engineering team for the U.S. Air Force F-16 airplane. She grew up in a small picturesque mountain town, where the mornings and evenings were taken up caring for a variety of pets, namely horses, goats, rabbits, dogs, cats.

At age four, she became a big sister to a beautiful little baby girl who would grow up to become her best friend. As her parents progressed in demanding careers, Krystina was training in ballet and equestrian sports. She and her sister were both homeschooled, and grew up involved in their local church community. In her late teens, Krystina dreamed of being married one day, a dream that became a reality when she met Stephen. An excitement arrived because of this blossoming long-distance relationship, but at the same time a longing to stay with the familiar.

In a naive and Divinely-inspired whirlwind wedding, she and Stephen got married when she was only 20. Less than 48 hours after entering into a marriage covenant, her whole life changed. A totally new life on the East Coast, a husband, and a journey she never expected was on the horizon. She is expectant for the blessing of motherhood, as her story unfolds from just desiring being a wife to feeling safe and secure enough to pursue motherhood. She loves hosting friends and family to whom she serves the most amazing delicious meals in their peaceful home; loves beautiful gardens, travel, and exploring new places with her beloved husband, Stephen.

The Sternes Programs

Join our Marriage & Relationship Community & Mastermind

You'll get access to our:

Community Platform

✓ Stay connected with our tribe on our online platform, where you can ask questions and get advice, insights, and prayer.

Monthly Group Web Conference Call

✓ Join a monthly group web conference call with encouragement, teaching, and prayer.

Weekly Video Teaching

✓ Get a weekly short video teaching from Stephen and Krystina focused on a biblical dating, marriage, conflict resolution, spiritual warfare, and a fulfilling marriage.

Additional benefits include:

✓ Discounted admission to our Grace Even After events and future offerings.

For more information please reach out to us at:
info@graceevenafter.com

www.graceevenafter.com